"This book contains fascinating and eye-opening information about our American beauty habits. Carolyn and Nicole have acted as our research assistants to open our eyes to the vanity of physical beauty and our hearts to the power of true beauty."

Dannah Gresh, best-selling author and creator of *Secret Keeper Girl*

"Our society is obsessed with the cult of beauty, and it is high time we recognize that this cult is nothing less than the worship of an idol. Carolyn Mahaney and Nicole Whitacre deliver a prophetic word against this idolatry, but more importantly, they rescue beauty from the clutches of the idol and present a biblical understanding of true beauty. This book should be read by every Christian woman and it should be put in the hands of every young girl as soon she can understand it. These gifted authors have not only written a book; they have launched a revolution."

R. Albert Mohler Jr. and Mary K. Mohler, President, The Southern Baptist Theological Seminary; and his wife, Mary, Director of the Seminary Wives Institute at The Southern Baptist Theological Seminary

"In a world where a woman's identity can easily be defined by how she looks, what she wears, or how she feels about herself, Carolyn Mahaney and Nicole Whitacre challenge us to something greater: the discovery of the truth about who we really are as God's crowning creation. Whether single, married, wife, mom, husband, father, brother, or boyfriend, *True Beauty* is a must-read. With so much wisdom, knowledge, and practical advice, this book will awaken your spirit to understand, to fight, to inspire, and to love."

Webb and Dowd Keith Simpson, Professional golfer, PGA Tour, and his wife and mother of three

"*'Delight in his flawless design'* is an incredible statement from the pages of this inspiring book. You will delight in the timeless principles and truths that, when applied, reflect the work of our wonderful Creator."

Karen Loritts, author; conference speaker; blogger, *MomLife Today*; mother of four and grandmother of eight

"Finally, a book about beauty that gets to the heart of the issue. As much as I'd like to blame my inadequacies on my clumpy mascara, outspoken personality, or spotty fitness routine, Carolyn and Nicole remind me that my problem is actually much deeper. It's not that I'm concerned too much or too little with my appearance; it's that I'm concerned with the wrong thing altogether. *True Beauty* puts in his rightful place the Source of all that is beautiful and good, and begs me to look there instead of my bathroom mirror. It's about time. How refreshing to finally get my eyes off myself!"

Lisa Anderson, Director of Young Adults, Focus on the Family; Host, *The Boundless Show*

"This is a wonderful, enjoyable, highly readable book that teaches God's true standards of beauty in contrast to the misleading standards promoted in popular culture today."

Wayne and Margaret Grudem, Research Professor of Theology and Biblical Studies, Phoenix Seminary. Wayne and Margaret have been married for forty-four years and have three children and three grandchildren.

"Combining the eminently practical with the deeply theological, Carolyn and Nicole give us a work that is both terrifically up-to-date and rooted in God's unchanging Word. With plenty of personal anecdotes and an inviting conversational style, *True Beauty* will meet women of all ages right where they are. But it won't leave them there! Carolyn and Nicole expose the lies we have picked up from the world and the half-truths that get passed along from well-meaning but misguided believers. We will recommend this book often and set it aside for our daughters to read as they grow up."

Kevin and Trisha DeYoung, Senior Pastor, University Reformed Church, East Lansing, Michigan. Kevin and Trisha have been married for twelve years and have six children.

"What woman hasn't struggled with the impossible standards of beauty bombarding her from magazine covers to her own mirror? We owe a debt of gratitude to Carolyn Mahaney and Nicole Whitacre for taking on this confusing 'crisis of beauty.' From self-loathing to apathetic acceptance, from closets to curbside, from plunging necklines to plastic surgery, the authors help us dig down to the real issue—our pursuit of self-glory. They show us the link between a woman's heart and her purity, modesty, and body image. *True Beauty* is theologically astute as well as practical, offering deliberate suggestions without being dictatorial, freeing us to develop our own Christ-honoring tastes as we see and savor authentic beauty in God and his Word. *True Beauty* will help every reader steward her beauty effectively for Christ. Read it. I can't wait to see the results!"

Jani Ortlund, Executive Vice President, Renewal Ministries; author, *Fearlessly Feminine* and *His Loving Law, Our Lasting Legacy*

"Finally . . . the book I've been wishing someone would write—a book that helps women like me who obsess about our own beauty (or more accurately, our lack thereof) to the detriment of our souls and our witness to the beauty and sufficiency of Christ. The answers Carolyn and Nicole put forward to our consuming and crippling desires to be beautiful on the world's terms are neither square nor simplistic but rather completely scriptural and deeply satisfying."

Nancy Guthrie, Bible Teacher; author, *Seeing Jesus in the Old Testament* Bible study series

"In a culture befuddled about femininity, *True Beauty* helps define what women are really looking for in their quest for that illusive thing called *beauty*. Carolyn and Nicole have tackled a subject that women everywhere care deeply about and really want to understand. Though the world has the microphone when it comes to peddling beauty, the promised payoff never satisfies. This book gives women a much-needed biblical response to the world's sales pitch."

Nancy Wilson, Pastor's wife; author, *Fruit of Her Hands; True Companion; Our Mother Tongue*

"A misunderstanding of what beauty truly is can tangle us up and keep us from walking in the freedom that all who trust in the Savior can enjoy. I recognized my own struggles through the pages of this book and was encouraged and renewed by the higher, broader, eternal, more beautiful vision of beauty it unfolded before my eyes: a vision made and grown and held together in Christ."

Kristyn Getty, Hymn-writer and recording artist

"Rare is the woman who doesn't struggle with her appearance. With four daughters and five granddaughters, we should know. This is a timely, relevant, and much-needed book, filled with gospel-fueled and theologically informed counsel. While relatively short, it contains a massive amount of hope and direction for women who confront the ongoing lies of our culture and their own hearts. Carolyn and Nicole address practical issues clearly without imposing personal standards, and share inspiring stories of women who have found grace in the midst of their battles. Whatever your season of life, *True Beauty* will lead you to behold and reflect the beauty of the Savior who is worthy of all our love and praise."

Bob and Julie Kauflin, Director, Sovereign Grace Music, and his wife

"This is more than a book on beauty or a book on how to see one's self as 'beautiful in God's eyes.' *True Beauty* points us to the beautiful One. The authors help us see God's pattern for reflecting the beauty of Christ in our hearts first and foremost, but also in the care of our bodies, in our fashion, and in other areas of life where beauty for its own sake tends to be a temptation. May all who read this book come away with greater desire to reflect the beauty of God in all of life."

Thabiti and Kristie Anyabwile, Senior Pastor, First Baptist Church of Grand Cayman, and his wife

"What a breath of fresh air this book brings to the complicated and far-too-often consuming relationship women have with beauty. Our culture is consumed with pursuing almost unattainable standards of appearance, and all of us have been influenced more than we know. This book reminds us of biblically sound, gospel-oriented truth. The authors help us see areas of self-absorption, and give us practical wisdom on how to grow in being absorbed with God and his glory. They help us examine our hearts and inspire us to grow beyond being women of 'good looks' to being women known for good works. I highly recommend this book for women of all ages, that we may become more oriented toward God's perspective on beauty, inward and outward."

Jodi Ware, Homemaker; Faculty Wife and Instructor in the Seminary Wives Institute, The Southern Baptist Theological Seminary

True
Beauty

Carolyn Mahaney
and Nicole Whitacre

CROSSWAY

WHEATON, ILLINOIS

Library of Congress Cataloging-in-Publication Data
Mahaney, Carolyn, 1955–
True beauty / Carolyn Mahaney and Nicole Whitacre.
　　　pages cm.
　　Includes bibliographical references and index.
　　ISBN 978-1-4335-4034-9
　　1. Aesthetics—Religious aspects—Christianity. I. Title.
BR115.A8M34　　　　　2014
248.8'43—dc23　　　　　　　　　　　　　　　2013030011

To the readers of the *girltalk* blog,
for sharing your stories
of beauty

Contents

Acknowledgments

We are grateful to partner once again with the wonderful folks at Crossway. Thank you to Ebeth Dennis who first had the idea for this book, to Justin Taylor and Tara Davis for shepherding it through the editing process, and to Josh Dennis and artist Wayne Brezinka for the cover art.

Thank you to Karen Ballinger, Vikki Cook, Kristin Jamieson, Betsy Ricucci, and Kathy Spiro for reading the manuscript and providing critique and encouragement. Special thanks to Candice Watters for your invaluable insight and edits.

To Nicole's children, Jack, Jude, Tori, and Sophie: thank you for praying for God to help Mommy and Mom-Mom finish the book.

To Janelle and Kristin—our fellow *girltalkers* and the best daughters and sisters ever—thanks for praying for and supporting us all the way to the finish line.

We could not have done this without our husbands, C. J. and Steve. You are our biggest encouragers, our most skilled editors, and our best friends. We love you!

Chapter One

True Beauty and Our Culture

"Growing up, all I could focus on was my nose."

Jasmine was ashamed of how prominent and ugly she thought her nose looked. From a young age she fixated on this one physical feature:

> I thought that my nose was the source of all of my problems with boys and life in general. I had zero experience with the opposite sex in any sort of romantic fashion. I was also not popular in school and had few close friends. I honestly believed that if I could get this "taken care of" my quality of life would be better.

So Jasmine decided to take care of her nose problem, hoping she would also solve her popularity problems, boy problems, and all-around quality of life problems:

> When I was eighteen, I chose to have an elective cosmetic surgical procedure—a rhinoplasty, which is a nose job. I can still vividly remember the day of my surgery, feeling scared and unsure of what the result would be. It was exciting to think that a whole new attractive future awaited me.

Beauty: Everywoman's Struggle

Jasmine is one of many women who wrote to tell me* their stories and struggles with beauty. When I asked for thoughts via our blog,

---

* We are a mother (Carolyn) and a daughter (Nicole) who wrote every word of *True Beauty* together. For the sake of simplicity and clarity, the personal comments and stories are from Carolyn.

girltalk, numerous women voiced similar difficulties with weight, self-image, comparison, and men.[1]

> My biggest struggle is being jealous of women who look like they just stepped out of a magazine.
>
> I am a young, single girl who struggles with accepting all aspects of my physical appearance.
>
> My self-image needs work.
>
> I used to be thin, but I've gained fifty pounds. I look in the mirror and wonder who I'm looking at.
>
> It's a struggle to feel attractive to my husband after pregnancy.
>
> I obsess daily about how I look.

Many women I heard from described struggles with beauty that are all-consuming. They obsess over a particular flaw or worry about their weight. Their life is a constant cycle of diet and exercise plans and new beauty treatments, which often end in failure and despair. They are full of self-loathing and depression about their appearance.

For other women, the struggle with beauty is low-grade but constant. There isn't one big thing; they just fret all the time about how they look. They check out their reflection when they pass a mirror and compare themselves to other women when they walk into a room. Their biggest question is: how much time, money, and effort are OK for a Christian woman to spend on beauty?

And then there are the mothers, struggling to raise young girls in a culture obsessed with beauty. They want to protect their daughters, but they feel powerless and desperate. I know the feeling. Having raised three daughters, I remember how difficult it was to help them resist the enormous pressure our culture places on young women to be beautiful.

As a pastor's wife, I have spoken to many women through the years about their trials and temptations with beauty. From these conversations and my own experiences, I know that as women our beauty struggles can range from subtle and nagging to life-dominating. But to one degree or another, the issue of beauty presses in on all of us.

Extraordinary Measures

Our struggles are magnified by a culture that is obsessed with physical beauty.

Every day we are bombarded with images of beauty: on television, movies, billboards, storefronts, and magazine ads, on our phones, tablets, and computer screens. These images tell us what we are supposed to look like, and they present a standard of beauty so narrow in its range that most of us feel unattractive by comparison.

What is this ideal standard of beauty? We must have a perfectly proportioned figure, exquisite facial features, flawless skin, and be free from defects or disabilities—not to mention that we must be young, or at least retain a youthful, healthy appearance.

And consider what it takes to achieve this look so highly valued by our culture. The fact is, most models and stars we see on magazines and movie screens spend countless hours on beauty treatments, undergo expensive procedures, including cosmetic surgery, and hire health professionals and physical trainers to help them achieve and maintain this perfect look.

One music star reportedly spends more than three hours of intense exercise per day doing yoga, Pilates, swimming, cycling, weight training, and working out on her exercise equipment.[2] Another well-known actress apparently pays over $20,000 a month to look good. Her costly beauty routine includes personal training, private yoga instruction, and "anti-cellulite spa sculpting" treatments. She also has a private chef who prepares organic, high protein, low-fat meals.[3]

These women are two examples, but no doubt they represent the investment of time and money required by the majority of the women who attempt to achieve our culture's standard of perfect beauty.

When is the last time you had three hours a day or $20,000 a month to spare on your beauty routine? Not in my lifetime! I daresay most of us do not have the time or financial resources to compete with actresses and models.

Not only do most of us lack the means to maintain our culture's ideal of beauty, in many cases the standard against which we are measuring ourselves isn't even real. Today many of the images we see online or in glossy magazines are photoshopped, retouched and smoothed, stretched and manipulated into a shape and appearance that is artificial and misleading.

Digital technology enables graphic artists to take a model and create a composite woman, an image that isn't even real, which provoked author Jean Kilbourne to lament:

> The image [of beauty] has become even more tyrannical and more perfect than ever before. . . . The pressure on girls which has existed for a long time is worse than ever because the ideal image now is so completely, inhumanly impossible to achieve.[4]

So the next time you see a picture of an impossibly skinny model or an unbelievably toned actress, remember, her portrait is most likely the final product of the labors of a talented graphic artist. Even the most beautiful woman cannot hope to attain our culture's tyrannical standard of beauty.

The Gospel according to Beauty

Despite the fact that the average woman can't pay out thousands of dollars per month on her beauty, or spend three hours a day exercising, or have a professional retouch all her photographs, women still chase this unattainable standard of beauty with a fury.

The statistics tell the story.

Few can afford $20,000 per month, but according to some figures, the average American woman spends a staggering $12,000 to $15,000 per year on beauty products and services.[5]

By one author's calculation, "in the United States more money is spent on beauty than on education and social services combined."[6]

That's not to mention the time it takes to apply all these products. The typical woman spends more than a year of her life—474 days on average—putting on cosmetics. That works out to one week per year,[7] and does not count the additional fifty-two days of our lives we spend removing said makeup.[8]

A tremendous amount of time and money is also spent on diet and exercise. The weight-loss industry in the United States pulls in a staggering $20 billion annually, and of the 108 million people on diets, 85 percent are women.[9]

Furthermore, twenty million American women will suffer from a clinically significant eating disorder in their lifetime.[10] According to one study, 65 percent of American women confess to an eating disorder.[11]

And cosmetic surgery continues to rise, increasing more than 80 percent in the past fifteen years, with Americans spending over $6 billion in 2012 alone.[12] This isn't a uniquely American problem: *The Times* of London forecasted that 80 percent of all women would have cosmetic surgery at some point.[13]

Dr. Albert Mohler sums up the situation: "An entire industry of billions of dollars is built upon the lie that one can buy enough or endure enough, suffer enough or apply enough, to be genuinely beautiful."[14]

Why are women so obsessed with physical beauty? Why do we go to extreme lengths to pursue our culture's elusive standard of perfection?

Women believe that beauty is essential to a happy life. We buy into our culture's message, often conveyed through media and advertising, that you have to be beautiful to be or get what you want. We think that if you are beautiful, you will achieve true romance and lasting love, that you will be popular and well-liked. We believe physical beauty is the key to self-confidence and self-worth, the only way to be satisfied, significant, and successful.

Like Jasmine, women often trace the source of their troubles back to a physical flaw or lack of beauty. We think that if we can only make ourselves more beautiful, then "a whole new attractive future" will lead to a whole new confident future, a whole new romantic future, a whole new happy future.

Our society has taken physical beauty and made it a god. The message of the gospel according to beauty is proclaimed in every advertisement and television show: *Beauty equals happiness. Beauty brings fulfillment. Beauty means success. Don't have physical beauty? You are condemned.*

Yet the message is a lie.

Physical beauty does not deliver as advertised. It does not ensure the satisfaction and success that the beguiling voices in our society have promised.

The Pretty (Big) Letdown

To validate the fact that physical beauty fails to bring happiness, consider two of the most beautiful women of modern times.

Princess Diana may have been the most photographed woman ever. She became a celebrity of unprecedented magnitude, yet she lived a troubled life. Her fairy-tale marriage to Prince Charles ended in divorce. Her subsequent relationships with other men were fraught with unhappiness. She admitted to persistent bouts of depression, chronic loneliness, ongoing bulimia, and acts of self-harm. Her life ended tragically when she was just thirty-six years old.

Another beautiful woman, actress Halle Berry, was the first African-American to represent the United States at the Miss World pageant. She has won numerous beauty titles and acting awards. But what does Halle Berry think about her beauty?

> Let me tell you something—being thought of as a beautiful woman has spared me nothing in life. No heartache, no trouble. Love has been difficult. Beauty is essentially meaningless and it is always transitory.[15]

All you have to do is glance at magazine covers in the grocery store aisle or click an online article to see heartbreaking stories about some of the most beautiful women in the world: unfaithful husbands and cheating boyfriends, eating disorders and stubborn depression, substance abuse and prison sentences.

But it is not only the stars who are disillusioned by the false promises of beauty; eventually, physical beauty will disappoint us all.

Jasmine's Story: What a New Face Didn't Fix

Jasmine learned this truth the hard way. Here's the conclusion to her story:

> The day the bandages came off, about two weeks later, was a day of great anxiety for me. After all, I was seeing my new *face* for the first time. It was almost like being reborn.
>
> To be honest, I still looked almost the same. The nose was distinctively different—but I was still the same old me. My personality hadn't changed.
>
> I would be lying if I said that my confidence didn't increase as a result of the procedure. My nose literally isn't the same shape or size that it used to be. But as for my new and exciting life, even cosmetic surgery didn't give me the satisfaction that I thought it would. Five years later, and I am still single.
>
> Every day I look in the mirror and see a nose that has been constructed. I haven't seen my actual God-given face in over five years. It brings me a bit of sadness, but my past is my past and there is nothing that I can do to change the shape of my nose now.

I rue the day that I have to tell my future husband that the face he loves so much is not the face that I was born with. It's the one secret that I keep in my back pocket, ashamed to share with friends and even some family members.

I paid one of the highest prices for the sake of beauty. And what did it bring me? Nothing.

Two Words Advertisers Don't Want You to Hear

Jasmine invested big. She was sure that physical beauty would provide the life she desired. But it didn't pay off. Jasmine's disappointment bears out the truth of what Scripture teaches: "Charm is deceitful, and beauty is vain" (Prov. 31:30). Charm—another word for outward form or physical appearance—is *deceitful*: "it promises a lifetime of happiness that it cannot deliver."[16]

Physical beauty deceives us by appearing to keep some of its promises in the short term. It delivers just enough to keep us hooked, to lead us on in thinking that it is a worthwhile investment of all our hope, time, money, and energy. For example, the pretty girls may get hired over the less attractive, and the sexy women get most of the attention from men. As Jasmine admitted, her new nose did give her more confidence.

But to put our trust in physical beauty is to fall for Satan's original Ponzi scheme (Gen. 3:6). The gospel according to physical beauty is nothing but a swindle. It may fulfill a temporary desire, but it will leave you desperate in the end. It may get you attention, but it won't bring you happiness. It may give you confidence, but it won't increase your true worth.

God's Word exposes the deceitfulness of physical beauty. Beauty does not provide the satisfaction every human heart is searching for. As Jasmine and Halle Barry can attest, a whole new attractive future does not lead to a whole new happy future; instead it "often end[s] in disappointment more bitter than words can tell."[17]

Not only is beauty deceitful, it is *vain*. It is like a vapor or a "puff of air."[18] All physical beauty vanishes over time. It doesn't last. Dr. David Powlison elaborates:

> Even women who succeed against the cultural ideal can do so for only a short window of time. Someday, everyone who lives long enough will look like Grandma or Great-Grandma: old, wrinkly, white-haired, frail, bent. You're in a race against time in which everyone loses. If you buy into the value system, someday you'll be cursed no matter what.[19]

Buy into the promise of physical beauty and you will be "cursed no matter what." Disappointment is guaranteed. Sickness, aging, and eventually death will see to that.

"Beauty—what a fading vanity it is!" exclaimed Charles Bridges. "One fit of sickness sweeps it away. Sorrow and care wither its charms. And even while it remains, it is little connected with happiness."[20]

And so, as a wise friend warns against a bad investment, Scripture urges us not to invest our hope in physical beauty. *Do not count on it for happiness, satisfaction, or the good things in life!* it tells us, because charm is deceitful and beauty is vain.

God's Word exposes the futility of physical beauty so we might avoid following the world over the cliff of obsession into the abyss of disappointment. Scripture has spoken the truth about beauty all along.

Don't Talk to Me about Inner Beauty

So what's a Christian girl to do? If physical beauty is deceitful and vain, is it wrong to try to look beautiful?

You may think you know what's coming next. This book is called *True Beauty*, so here's the part where I tell you to forget about looking good and focus on inner beauty, right? Richelle was so concerned she sent me this request:

Please don't base your book off 1 Peter 3:4: "But let your adorning be the hidden person of the heart with the imperishable beauty of a gentle and quiet spirit, which in God's sight is very precious." This verse, misapplied in my life, left me very confused, hurt, and hidden for almost fifteen years.

Many women feel burned by a "Christian" message that has—often with the best of intentions—misinterpreted passages on beauty or been used to impose personal preferences. Like Richelle, women sometimes feel confused and conflicted by a message about beauty they have been told is biblical.

But perhaps you have never really heard what the Bible has to say about beauty, or you've assumed it is irrelevant, only applicable to women who lived in biblical times. Or maybe you've heard it all before—from your parents and your pastors—and you're not interested in the same old lecture.

Maybe you have tried to apply God's Word to your beauty struggles and you feel like it hasn't worked for you. It hasn't helped you lose weight or climb out of your depression or overcome your insecurities. So you've given up on the Bible as a source of real, practical help when it comes to beauty.

But God's Word is not outdated or shortsighted. Scripture doesn't fail to answer our questions or address our struggles. The Bible actually has a surprising amount to say about beauty. For instance, Scripture tells us that God delights in beauty—a theme we will return to throughout the book. The Bible does not say physical beauty is bad or that it is sinful to make ourselves beautiful. Instead, it tells us how to make ourselves truly beautiful.

The Beautiful Truth about True Beauty

God is our Creator. He "knows our frame" (Ps. 103:14), and he is acquainted with all our ways (Ps. 139:3), including our desires and difficulties as they relate to beauty.

He is not surprised or flummoxed by the mess our culture has gotten itself into. He doesn't need to revise his counsel based on the latest health study or issue a press release in response to the ever-deepening crisis among teenage girls.

God's Word exposes the distortion of beauty in our culture. It diagnoses our problems with beauty (even when we don't think we have any) and offers the only solution.

Scripture speaks truth about beauty for every one of us, whether we have failed to stick with our new diet or been conned into buying another worthless anti-aging cream; whether we feel guilty for our weekend shopping spree, or embarrassed by a bad hair day; whether we are vain and self-absorbed, or fed up with our insecurities. In all our struggles with beauty, whether nagging or consuming, God has provided the wisdom that we need in his eternal Word.

Scripture shows us what true beauty is and how to become truly beautiful. Above all, Scripture reveals our beautiful Savior, who had "no beauty that we should desire him" (Isa. 53:2) but who hung bloodied on a cross for the ugliest of our sins.

The gospel of Jesus Christ really does redeem everything, including beauty. It really does reach into the heart of "if only I could get this taken care of" and takes care of it. Our beauty crisis is no match for the truth of God's Word.

And so this simple book has a modest aim: to point you to true beauty in the Bible.

I am not writing this book because I am an expert in the beauty industry. I am not a psychologist or a dietician or a cosmetologist. I have not discovered a beauty secret or developed a breakthrough weight-loss program. And I don't have a dramatic makeover story to tell. I'm just an average woman who has common struggles with how I look.

But my confidence rests entirely on the Word of God, its clarity and sufficiency, its power and purpose. I believe Scripture is the only hope to transform our beauty crisis.

As a pastor's wife for over thirty-five years, I have walked with many women as they have struggled with their appearance: the teenage girl with acne, the wife whose husband is looking at pornography, the friend caught in the vice grip of an eating disorder, the woman struggling with a negative body image.

But I have also watched these women put their trust in God's Word and bravely defy the world's lies about beauty. And I have witnessed the truth of God's Word restore their lives and their joy, and make them beautiful.

My hope is that you too will be encouraged to bring every question about beauty and every struggle with your appearance to God's Word. My prayer is that you will trust in his Word and submit to his Word, finding hope, freedom, and delight in the beauty of his truth.

Only God's Word can promise a beauty as supernatural as it is satisfying, as attainable as it is lasting; a beauty that blesses and does not curse; a beauty that is precious, not worthless, that leads to happiness instead of heartache; a beauty that grows more becoming even as you become more beautiful.

Scripture is true and tells the truth. It alone reveals true beauty.

All flesh is grass,
and all its beauty is like the flower of the field.
The grass withers, the flower fades . . .
but the word of our God will stand forever. (Isa. 40:6–8)

Chapter Two

True Beauty and Our God

Would the most beautiful woman please come forward?

Elsie Scheel may not be whom you were expecting. Hailing from Brooklyn and weighing 171 pounds, she was five feet seven inches tall, making her a size 12/14 skirt at today's Banana Republic. *The New York Times* anointed her "the most nearly perfect physical specimen of womanhood."[1]

The year was 1912.

Fast forward a few decades and you'll find numerous ads from the 1930s, '40s, and '50s promoting weight-gain products for the much-pitied "Girls With 'Naturally Skinny' Figures" who, for some reason, couldn't seem to attract a date. The reason? "Skinny girls are not glamour girls."[2]

Yes, you read that correctly. It's incomprehensible to our current ideal of beauty.

My first thought when I hear stories like this is, *I am a woman untimely born! At some moment and at some place in history, my body type might have been considered "most nearly perfect." Why couldn't I have been born then and there?*

But, alas, I am a fifty-something woman in the early twenty-first century, and the thought of being nominated as the most beautiful woman only makes me laugh.

Here Today, Gone Tomorrow

Not only has the ideal image of beauty morphed through the decades and centuries, it also changes rapidly year to year, from one fashion season to another. The clothes, cosmetics, and hairstyles that were popular a few months ago may be out of style today. The rules of beauty in our modern culture are transient, fickle, and elusive.

Each New Year, *The Washington Post* reminds us of the fickleness of fashion and other petty preferences with its annual "In/Out List": a compilation of public figures, phrases, fashions, foods, drinks, sports, and activities that were popular last year and *not* popular this year.[3] These "ins" and "outs" showcase a standard of beauty in our society that is in constant flux.

I don't know about you, but I'd like the fashions to hold still, even if only for a few minutes, thank you very much. For no matter how much time and money we spend trying to keep up on the latest trends, they are all going to change really soon. No matter how hard we try to fit into the current ideal of beauty, we often feel like we will never measure up.

Whether you are a thirteen-year-old agonizing over what the other girls will be wearing back to school this year or a fifty-eight-year-old who can't figure out the latest way to tie a scarf, we all feel the pangs of coming up short of beautiful. We all long for a standard of beauty we can actually attain.

But we don't have to accept our culture's ever-changing and ever-more-tyrannical definition of beauty. As women transformed by the gospel of Jesus Christ, we can know a standard of beauty that never changes and is attainable by us all. We can be free to enjoy style and beauty as God always intended.

To do so, we must discover how God defines beauty. What is *true* beauty?

The Sum of All Things Beautiful, and Then Some

To find true beauty, we have to rewind through centuries of changing fashion to the source: the "foundation and fountain" of all that is beautiful.[4] The Bible shows us true beauty. It reveals God as *the* beautiful One. Long before the ins and outs of changing fashion, God existed in perfect beauty. He is the ultimate, unchanging, eternal standard of beauty. He is the Author, Creator, and Bestower of beauty. His beauty transcends time and culture. It never changes and never fades. In order to know what true beauty is, we must see God.

Imagine you could create a montage of every beautiful thing you have ever seen or wished for. Even so, you have not yet begun to comprehend the beauty of God. He is "the sum of all desirable qualities."[5]

More desirable than a child's ice cream cone topped with all her favorite flavors, more wonderful than a dream vacation that never ends, God's beauty is the sum total of every desirable thing we can imagine, and then his beauty soars beyond our greatest imaginings.

Let us marvel for a moment at the beauty of God.

God's beauty is *eternal*. While earthly beauty fades away, God's beauty is forever. It always was and it always will be. God's beauty is outside and above time and trends. With God "there is no variation or shadow due to change" (James 1:17).

God's *loveliness* is seen in creation, but it is only a dim reflection of his stunning glory. His attractiveness is indescribable. His appearance is "like the sun shining in full strength" (Rev. 1:16).

God's *power* topples nations and flashes lightning. He rules the oceans and the galaxies and he holds every man's heart in his hands. No prince or problem is a match for the beauty of God's power (Job 36:30; Prov. 21:1).

God's *wisdom* means that he knows all things, first to last. He never discovers or learns. Every possible outcome has its conclusion in him. He knows what is best and most beautiful in every situation, and causes all things to work infallibly for his glory (Job 12:13).

God's *holiness* is what the angels sing of as they gaze unceasingly upon the beauty of the Lord: "Holy, holy, holy, is the Lord

God Almighty" (Rev. 4:8). Not only is he pure and undefiled by sin, he is set apart from us in every way. His beauty is wholly uncorrupted.

God's *goodness* sends rain on the evil and the good. Every happy moment, every treasured gift, every blessing flows straight from the beautiful goodness of our God. The beauty of his goodness is most clearly seen in his plan of salvation (Ps. 119:68).

God's *justice* is beautifully strong, steadfast, and immovable. It is never broken or convoluted. It never fails, "for all his ways are justice" (Deut. 32:4).

And that's the short list! No wonder C. S. Lewis wrote, "The sweetest thing in all my life has been the longing . . . to find the place where all the beauty came from."[6]

Frankly, though, we're not always that interested in God's beauty, are we? It's great quiet time contemplation, but it can feel remote and disconnected from our body issues and our wardrobe fails, our hair troubles and our complexion flaws, our acne and our aging. We often fail to see what the beauty of God has to do with our weekend shopping trip or our next visit to the salon.

But a vision of God's beauty changes how we dress and exercise and eat. God's beauty reshapes our shopping and showering and showing off. It upends and undoes all our preferences about what is pretty and what is not. A glimpse of God's beauty makes all the difference in what we see when we look in the mirror.

Once we see God's beauty, we will never see beauty the same way again.

True beauty is to behold and reflect the beauty of God.

A Taste for Beauty

God could have spent eternity enjoying his beauty exclusively in the communion of the Trinity. But he went public with his beauty and poured forth his glory in the astonishing act of creation.[7]

He scattered the roaring waters and spread the sparkling sand.

He painted fields of emerald green and topped the hills with wooly flocks. He placed starfish on the murky bottom of the sea and commanded the sun to shine. He coaxed an elegant flower from the ground and started the river meandering. He billowed the clouds and bejeweled the night sky.

"It is good," he said when he had finished (Gen. 1:31), which can also mean: It is *beautiful*.[8] Our beautiful God created a beautiful world. He made "everything beautiful in its time" (Eccles. 3:11).

And "everything beautiful" includes us! Our beautiful Creator made us in his image. He made both male and female to be like him and to represent him.[9] We all bear the unmistakable stamp of his beauty. "According to the Bible, every single human being is made in the image of God, and is thus, for this reason alone, truly beautiful" asserts Albert Mohler.[10]

Who me? Truly beautiful?

Many of us struggle to believe this is true. But we have been created in God's beautiful image, and it is *for this reason alone* that we are truly beautiful. We are not beautiful because we fit the popular ideal of beauty, and we are not ugly or unattractive because we don't measure up. Our beauty as human beings is not derived from ourselves. It comes from our beautiful God.

Here is the fixed standard of beauty in our fickle culture. No matter our body type, age, skin color, height, or weight, whether we have a disability or deformity, whether or not we meet the current cultural standard, we are all beautiful because we have been created in the image of God. This levels the playing field. It radically redefines physical beauty. And it pulls our gaze away from ourselves and onto our beautiful God.

Not only did God create us in the image of his beauty, he implanted in each of us a desire for beauty: "The longing for beauty, along with an ability to recognize and experience it, exists within every human being" because it comes from God.[11] It "is something of great value in human and spiritual experience."[12]

This is why we instinctively beautify our space and our looks. It's why we freshen a room with flowers or refresh our lipstick. Our propensity to make things beautiful is good because it is from God. "This taste [for beauty]" writes John Angell James, "is in its own nature an imitation of the workmanship of God, who 'by his Spirit has *garnished* the heavens,' and covered the earth with beauty."[13]

Here again God's beauty redirects how we pursue beauty. It is not sinful or shameful to improve our appearance. Unloveliness is not next to godliness. God, our Creator, is the beautiful One. He made us beautiful, and our "taste for beauty" comes from him.

Taste Ruined, but God . . .

God set a taste for beauty in the heart of man and then set him in a beautiful garden to enjoy that beauty. But mankind wasn't long for paradise. Adam sinned, and in him, so did we all (Rom. 5:12).

Sin blinded us to the beauty of God, and when we lost sight of his beauty, we lost interest. His wisdom and goodness no longer moved us to worship. We could not bask in his loveliness or marvel at his power. The true beauty of the beautiful One now seemed boring at best.

Without a clear vision of the beauty of God, our perspective of earthly beauty became twisted and distorted. Instead of seeing the beauty of the image of God in the mirror, we could only see flaws. Rather than seeing the beauty of God in others, we envied and criticized.

And sin corrupted our taste for beauty. Instead of delighting in God's beauty, we put our hope in physical beauty and sought pleasure in that which was ugly and sinful. No more could we savor true beauty (Rom. 1:18–23). We lost our taste for God's beauty and all became bitter.

But in the most stunning act of beauty, unparalleled in all of human history, God displayed his love by sending his Son to bear his wrath on the cross for our sin. And through his death and resurrection, he made it possible for us to see and savor true beauty once again. In the person of Jesus Christ and his substitutionary sacrifice, we most clearly see the beauty of God here on earth.

Taste Refashioned

If God the Father is "the foundation and fountain" of beauty, then Jesus is the breathtaking display of the Father's beauty. He is the most visible expression of the beauty of God. "He is the radiance of the glory of God" (Heb. 1:3).

Jesus is "always surprising you and taking your breath away," quotes Tim Keller, "because he is incomparably better than you could imagine for yourself":[14]

> He has tenderness without weakness. Strength without harshness. Humility without the slightest lack of confidence. Unhesitating authority with a complete lack of self-absorption. Holiness and unbending convictions without the lack of approachability. Power without insensitivity. I once heard a preacher say, "No one has yet discovered the word Jesus ought to have said. He is full of surprises, but they are all the surprises of perfection."[15]

Jesus, the One who had "no beauty that we should desire him," is at the same time the most glorious expression of the beauty of God on earth (Isa. 53:2). He is the pinnacle of perfect beauty. And in dying for our sins on the cross, Jesus displayed his extravagant love, in all its beauty:

> Crown him the Lord of love;
>   behold his hands and side,
> those wounds, yet visible above,
>   in beauty glorified.[16]

If we have repented and believed in Jesus, part of God's saving power is to restore our vision and reawaken an appreciation for true beauty. Even now, the Holy Spirit is at work inside of us, refashioning our taste for beauty, reshaping our opinions about beauty, and reviving our desires for true beauty. The glorious gospel of Jesus Christ makes it possible for us to once again revel in true beauty and to reflect it in our lives.

How then can we allow the world to define beauty for us? As women transformed by the gospel, we must not exalt the current ideal of physical beauty over the eternal standard of God's beauty in Jesus Christ. Our taste for beauty and our opinions about beauty should, at every point, be allied to the beauty of God. Because our taste for beauty comes from him in the beginning, it is accountable to him in the end.

The gospel has laid double claim to our taste for beauty: first through creation and again through redemption.

Do We Like Beauty That Is Godlike?

We need to ask ourselves: "Do my beauty tastes—what I like and dislike—reflect and honor the beauty of God?"

Maybe you have never asked this question before; maybe you've never really thought about your tastes being accountable to God one way or another. Or maybe you never even stopped to consider who or what is shaping your beauty preferences. You just like what you like.

However, our taste for beauty is always being molded. The media we consume, the actresses we admire, the role models we look to, the people we relate with—all are constantly informing our ideas and preferences about beauty. The ever-changing cultural trends have a profound influence on our aesthetic sensibilities.

Think about it: our most common reaction to old photographs is to laugh at our clothes or hairstyle. *I can't believe I actually wore that shirt! Just look at my hair!* Ironically, we probably thought we looked pretty good at the time. Moments like these often reveal how influenced we are by whatever is the latest style.

Not that we like to think so. We prefer the illusion that our tastes are personal, that our style reflects our own unique character and artistic sense. Truth is, our likes and dislikes are often shaped by popular culture more than we care to admit. For myself, I realize that I have often been unaware of just how profoundly the culture affects my taste for beauty.

As Christians, we should be alert to what is shaping our beauty preferences. We must not allow the world to press us into its beauty mold. The Creator, and not the creatures, should direct our taste for beauty.

In the words of Wayne Grudem, we must "refuse to accept our society's definition of beauty, or even the definitions that we ourselves may have worked with previously and decide that that which is truly beautiful is the character of God himself."[17] Let's consider the qualities of God's beauty and evaluate our own taste for beauty in light of his character.

Take, for example, God's *holiness*. If God is pure and cannot look on sin, then our style preferences should be in harmony with this aspect of his beauty. If we admire and enjoy clothing that is immodest, provocative, or seductive, then our tastes belie the beauty of God's holiness. Rather, the Christian woman should value a style and appearance that represents the purity and holiness of God.

God's *wisdom* has great bearing on our taste for beauty. In his perfect wisdom he has made men and women to reflect his image in equal and yet distinctly different ways. So if we, as women, prefer a masculine style or scorn femininity in our dress and demeanor, we reject the wisdom of God. We show our delight in God's good plan when we are grateful to be and look like a woman.

And what does our preferred style say about the beauty of God's *eternity*? Clothing and accessories that glorify death, despair, and spiritual darkness speak a message contrary to the eternal character of God. But a Christian woman's taste for beauty should reflect and proclaim the joy of eternal life through Jesus Christ.

Do our clothes and demeanor represent the *loveliness* of Christ? Do they display his *power* over sin and selfishness? Does our sense of style reflect humility in response to his *greatness*? Does thankfulness for his *goodness* inform our fashion sense? Let's consider how God's beauty is reflected in every aspect of our style.

Bringing our tastes in line with the beauty of God is not restrictive or repressive. An appreciation of God's beauty actually deepens and enhances our taste for beauty; it does not dampen or hinder it. In keeping with the multifaceted beauty of God, the styles that reflect his character may be wonderfully diverse.

God's beauty raises our tastes above petty preferences. Lovely comes in many shapes, styles, and colors, as long as our tastes are bent toward reflecting the loveliness of Christ. Femininity can be expressed in a variety of fashions and yet still speak of God's beautiful wisdom. God's goodness may be glorified by a style that is soft and simple or bold and vibrant, all reflecting the beauty of his character.

The beauty of God is a fixed reference point amidst fluctuating style. While my personal fashion preferences have changed from a few years ago, and will no doubt be different in a few years' time, the beauty of God's holiness, power, and wisdom should be constantly reflected in my style.

Transforming Taste

If we realize that our taste for beauty needs realignment, what do we do? Scripture provides a simple paradigm for change:

> Do not be conformed to this world, but be transformed by the renewal of your mind, that by testing you may discern what is the will of God, what is good and acceptable and perfect. (Rom. 12:2)

Do not be conformed. Let's evaluate our taste for beauty and ask: "Who or what influences my sense of style?" and "In what ways does the ungodly culture shape my fashion preferences?" If necessary, let's take deliberate steps to limit worldly influences on our taste for beauty: cancel the subscription, change the channel, spend less time browsing online, or walk past the store.

Be transformed. To develop an ever-deepening taste for the beauty of God, spend time studying his beauty. *Look* for illustrations of the beauty of God in your daily Bible reading. *Study* his beautiful attributes: his holiness, his loveliness, and his power, all revealed most clearly in Jesus Christ. *Ask* yourself how these qualities should shape your taste for beauty. *Pray* that God would open your eyes to see his beauty and to reflect it in your style.

The more we see God's beauty, the more our taste for beauty will be transformed.

True Beauty

The gospel of Jesus Christ transforms our taste for beauty, but that is just the beginning. In this book we will discover how the beauty of God shapes all of what we believe and how we pursue beauty.

True beauty is to behold and reflect the beauty of God.

When we *behold* God's beauty, we become like him. The truly beautiful woman is the one who contemplates the beauty of God. As she worships him for his loveliness, power, holiness, and goodness, she is changed. By the power of the Holy Spirit, her life radiates the beauty of the gospel.

And the beautiful woman is deliberate to *reflect* the beauty of God in every aspect of her life, representing him in her appearance and her character. She consciously seeks to glorify God in her heart attitude, how she cares for her body, what she wears, and how she makes herself beautiful.

As we have already begun, let us continue to learn how we can behold and reflect God's true beauty in our lives.

For how great is his goodness, and how great his beauty! (Zech. 9:17)

Chapter Three

True Beauty and Our Hearts

April and Eva are very different women, but they have more in common with each other—and with you and me—than it might appear at first.

Meet April. Anxiety about her appearance is a perpetual problem:

> When I was younger, I struggled with my appearance and wanting to measure up and fit in—but I always felt like I fell terribly short. I felt I needed to look a certain way for someone to love me. So when the Lord blessed me with a godly husband who loved me, I truly thought my struggle was over. In some ways it was, but in other ways it wasn't.
>
> Now I struggle with my appearance in different ways. I want to look mature and be respected. I want to fit in with other moms. But I feel like I fall terribly short, again. So what should I do? Should I go out and buy a whole new wardrobe, get a fun hairstyle, go back to uncomfortable contacts, wear make-up all the time?
>
> I am struggling with all this, while trying to train up my little girl in the ways of the Lord. She has recently wanted her hair done just like another girl at school, and wanted to wear more dresses because they make her pretty.
>
> But when I try to talk with her about true beauty, I stumble over my words. Why? Because I have a hard time with the subject myself. It is something I have struggled with my whole life and so desperately want to be free from.

April wants to measure up and fit in. She wants to be attractive and accepted. Yet she feels like she is constantly falling short. The nagging internal murmurings of inadequacy and self-doubt hang around her like a damp fog and never seem to lift.

Something tells her it shouldn't be like this. *Am I really supposed to go through life constantly struggling with my appearance? As a grown woman, shouldn't I be over this by now?*

The cycle seems set to repeat in her little girl's life. April wishes she could spare her daughter the same struggles. If only she knew what to do.

Good Advice Gone Bad

Many would diagnose April with having low self-esteem. They would want her to know: *You are beautiful just the way you are.* Caring and concerned individuals would try to convince April that she does measure up. All she needs to do is ignore the negative messages about beauty in our culture and believe that she is special and beautiful.

Sincere Christians often take this one step further. *You are beautiful just the way you are because God made you and he thinks you are beautiful.* If you believe this is true, you will feel better about yourself, the thinking goes.

Now, as we learned in the previous chapter, there are important truths embedded in this counsel. The dignity of every human being made in the image of God means we all have an inherent beauty.

But this glorious truth often doesn't help us when we feel unattractive or anxious about our appearance. For me, I can convince myself that I am beautiful for only so long. All it takes is for my scale to register a few extra pounds or to walk past a woman who is younger and prettier than me, and that bubble bursts quickly.

Why doesn't this truth stick? Why doesn't this astounding knowledge—that we are beautiful because we are made in the image of God—eradicate, once and for all, our feelings of inadequacy and self-doubt?

One reason is that we often mistakenly turn this truth about God into clichés about us. When we turn the spotlight away from God and onto ourselves, we twist the truth. So "*God is beautiful and made us in his image*" becomes "*You are beautiful because God created you.*" Herein lies the flaw in the advice commonly given to someone like April: it starts and ends with us.

When we focus on ourselves, we're only compounding the problem. That's because self-focus *is* our problem. Sagging self-confidence is often a preoccupation with *self*; struggles with comparison, measuring up, and fitting in reveal our *self*-absorption. "Low self-esteem usually means that I think too highly of myself," explains Ed Welch. "I'm too self-involved, I feel I deserve better than what I have. The reason I feel bad about myself is that I aspire to something more. I want just a few minutes of greatness."[1]

Feelings of inadequacy about our appearance often arise because we feel we deserve better than what we have. Take April, for instance. Even after God blesses her with a husband who loves her just the way she is, her struggles with beauty resurface. She aspires to something more.

We may not feel like we're grasping at greatness—we just want to fit in with the other moms or the popular girls at school—but then again, we never seem to be liked enough or included enough to make us happy. We never get what we think we deserve.

This is why our beauty struggles seem set on repeat: self is never satisfied. But there is hope for April, for you, and for me. When we accurately diagnose our struggles with beauty, we can break free from this destructive cycle.

How Much Vanity Is Too Much Vanity?

Eva has a problem with beauty, too. At first glance, her problem seems to be the opposite of April's struggle. "I am the epitome of a vain person," writes Eva:

This is my own fault and never would I want to blame somebody else for my sin. With that being said, my vanity was fueled by growing up in a family that gave a lot of emphasis to what one looked like. We had mirrors in every room! I counted one day that we had seventeen large mirrors and a mirrored wall in our small house. As a family we were and still are obsessed about how we look. My mother has since had plastic surgery, my brother and father spend exorbitant amounts of money on clothes, and then there is me, the worst of them all. I obsess daily about how I look. Before going to my university, I put on my make-up, making sure it is perfect. I fix my hair and my clothes so that other people will look at me and think "Oh, she looks pretty." I am far too concerned with how I look and how others view me.

If concern about how we look and how others view us makes us "the epitome of a vain person," then a bunch of us are going to have to, however sheepishly, raise our hands. But what is the definition of vanity exactly? How do I know for sure if I am being vain?

Because the answer isn't always clear, we invent arbitrary guidelines to satisfy our conscience: it isn't vanity as long as I don't buy too many shoes or spend too much time in front of the mirror or act like *she* does. We all know those women who are obsessed with looking beautiful and stylish—the always-exercising, always-shopping, always-eating-right, never-wearing-the-same-thing-twice kind of woman—and if we aren't like that, we figure we must be OK.

But it isn't only the woman who flaunts her good looks who is vain. We are all susceptible, whether we grew up in a house with seventeen mirrors or one. To be vain is to take pride in our looks, or an aspect of our appearance, and endeavor to get attention, approval, and affirmation, even in small or subtle ways.

If we get dressed or apply our make-up in order to elicit compliments, if we exercise and diet so people will think we look good, if we fantasize about being thought of as attractive, we are expressing vanity.

For all of us, vanity is not measured primarily by hours in front of the mirror or the size of our shoe collection (although these may be indicators), but by our motivation for buying the shoes and spending the mirror time.

While most of us don't admit our vanity as humbly as Eva, even to ourselves, we all desire attention and approval for how we look. Surely Eva is not "the worst of them all."

The End for Which God Created Woman

So what does the woman with low self-esteem have in common with the woman struggling with vanity? At first glance, they seem nothing alike.

But the truth is, they both want attention and approval for how they look. Low self-esteem is simply the flip side of vanity: pride disappointed, approval unattained. And both sides of vanity are serious because of the worth and value of the One who deserves all attention and admiration.

When God created us in his image, made us beautiful, and gave us a taste for beauty to enjoy this beautiful world, it was not so that we could squander our time trying to measure up and fit in or so we could style our hair and apply our makeup just so that others would say, "Oh, isn't she pretty!"

God made us for *his* glory. We were created to worship, delight in, and bring glory to our beautiful God. "He has made [us] for this very end" wrote Jonathan Edwards, "to think and be astonished [at] his glorious perfections."[2]

The child who learns his catechism knows that "man's chief end is to *glorify* God, and to enjoy him forever."[3] This is why Scripture repeatedly exhorts us to "ascribe to the LORD the glory due his name; worship the LORD in the splendor of holiness" (Ps. 29:2); and "sing the glory of his name; give to him glorious praise!" (Ps. 66:2).

Glory is the Lord's and his alone. "My glory I will not give to another" (Isa. 48:11), he declares. All of Scripture rings with this theme. This is what we were made for. This is our purpose in life: to bring glory to our beautiful God.

But the inescapable truth is this: when we try to get attention for our own beauty, we cease to give God glory for his beauty.

"Sin makes us glory thieves," explains Paul Tripp:

> There is probably not a day when we do not plot to steal glory that rightfully belongs to the Lord. . . . Sin causes us to steal the story and rewrite it with ourselves as the lead, and with our lives at center stage. But there is only one stage and it belongs to the Lord. Any attempt to put ourselves in his place puts us in a war with him. It is an intensely vertical war, a fight for divine glory, a plot to take the very position of God. It is the drama that lies behind every sad earthly drama. Sin has made us glory robbers.[4]

At the bottom of our beauty struggles is "a fight for divine glory." The vain, confident woman and the insecure, depressed woman both want God's glory for themselves, for their own beauty. They want center stage. And so do we all.

It is as if we are jumping up and down, waving our hands and shouting in hopes that everyone in the gallery will turn away from the main attraction—our beautiful God—and look at us. Or, we are moping in the corner because they didn't look. In both cases, we are grasping for glory that is God's alone.

Some of us may parade our beauty for our own glory. Some of us may brood and worry over glory unattained. Most of us do a little of both. But whenever we try to get attention and admiration for our own beauty—whether or not we are successful—we are robbing God of the glory that only he deserves.

The Path to Sweet Contentment

Glory thieves? Really? Maybe this sounds a bit extreme, even a little harsh. Do we really apply makeup in order to deliberately rob God of glory or get dressed so we can steal the show from God?

While every woman whose heart has been transformed by the gospel desires to glorify God with her life, we are all susceptible to the temptations of vanity and self-focus. Unmasking our motives as "glory thieves" helps us to make sense of it all. When we become conscious of our self-focus, or feel guilt because of our vanity, this is our conscience at work. These are indicators from the Holy Spirit that something is wrong. As Christians, we can no longer rob God of glory and feel good about it. That's a good thing!

When we see our problem for what it is, we can begin to take steps in the right direction. We can put aside self-glory and devote our beauty efforts toward their original purpose: "He who glories, let him glory in the Lord" (1 Cor. 1:31 NKJV).

For many years I did not understand God's truth about my beauty struggles. In high school, I felt sorry for myself if I wasn't included in the most popular crowd, or when my parents didn't have enough money for me to keep up with the latest styles.

Even as a grown woman, I have often compared myself to others and have been overly concerned about my appearance. Looking back, I can see that my preoccupation with how I looked was nothing more than vanity and self-absorption. Of course I still struggle with temptations to self-glory, but understanding the true nature of my beauty struggle helps me to detect sin earlier and resist it more effectively.

So how can we discern self-glorifying motives that have infiltrated our beauty pursuit? J. I. Packer offers this helpful diagnostic:

> The test is to ask yourself how pleased, or how displeased, you become if God is praised while you are not, and equally if you are praised while God is not. The mature Christian is content

not to have glory given to him, but it troubles him if men are not glorifying God.[5]

This is sweet contentment: untroubled by the attention and approval of others, concerned only for the renown of God's beauty.

Free Indeed

Hopefully, we are beginning to see a pathway out of our beauty struggles.

The "you are beautiful just the way you are" advice is inadequate to break the depressing cycle of low self-esteem because it fails to address our real problem. And superficial rules do nothing to curb our vanity and quiet our conscience.

But when we understand that our self-focus and vanity is worse than we thought—robbing God of glory—then we can take steps of repentance and experience freedom from our struggles with beauty. Remember: only the gospel of Jesus Christ can set us free. It is only through the atoning death of our Savior that we can be forgiven of "glory robbing" and receive power to glory in the beauty of God.

Our beautiful Savior came to free us from ourselves: "And he died for all, that those who live might no longer live for themselves but for him who for their sake died and was raised" (2 Cor. 5:15). When we abandon our pursuit of self-glory, we will know the happiness and contentment that accompanies true freedom. C. S. Lewis put it this way:

> As long as we have the itch of self-regard we shall want the pleasure of self-approval: but the happiest moments are those when we forget our precious selves and have neither, but have everything else (God, our fellow-humans, animals, the garden & the sky) instead.[6]

Another British thinker, G. K. Chesterton, observed the same problem in humanity as Lewis, and likewise exulted in the grace of God that gives us freedom from selfishness and pride:

> How much larger your life would be if your self could become smaller in it. . . . You would break out of this tiny and tawdry theatre in which your own little plot is always being played, and you would find yourself under a freer sky. . . . How much happier you would be, how much more of you there would be, if the hammer of a higher God could smash your small cosmos, scattering the stars like spangles, and leave you in the open, free like other men to look up.[7]

The Antidote to Self-Glory

So how do we forget our precious selves and get to this freer sky? We behold the beauty of God. David modeled this for us in the Psalms:

> One thing have I asked of the LORD,
>   that will I seek after:
> that I may dwell in the house of the LORD
>   all the days of my life,
> *to gaze upon the beauty of the LORD*
>   and to inquire in his temple. (Ps. 27:4)

Gazing upon the beauty of the Lord is the antidote to self-glory. Ed Welch explains:

> If only we could have something big enough, powerful enough, attractive enough to take our attention away from our self just for a moment, to put our attention somewhere else. Sometimes I think one of the great lessons of the gospel in my own life is that I can just think less frequently about myself.
>
> Consider what it would be like to be in Revelation chapter 4 where you find yourself in the throne room of God. You know what's going to happen when you are in the throne room of God? You are not going to be thinking about your

personal appearance. We're not going to be thinking about our hair. We're not going to be thinking about our weight. Instead, our attention is going to be drawn to the One who is truly beautiful. . . . One of the privileges of heaven is that we'll gaze at the throne and see new facets of beauty day after day after day.[8]

The gospel frees us to think less frequently about ourselves. We don't have to wait until our Revelation 4 moment in heaven. We can, and we must, like David, seek to behold God's beauty *all the days of our lives.* It is this deliberate, daily decision to gaze upon his beauty where change takes place. This is how we start to shed our preoccupation with ourselves and with our own beauty.

So, as I suggested in the previous chapter, take time in your daily Bible reading to find one aspect of God's beauty upon which to meditate. Remembering that he is "the sum of all desirable qualities," ask yourself, which of God's desirable qualities are displayed in this passage?

Write the verse on an index card. Send it as a text or e-mail to yourself. Set it as your laptop wallpaper. Keep it handy. Seize spare moments throughout the day to behold the beauty of God, to thank him for his goodness or praise him for his holiness, to worship him for his power and his loveliness.

And you know what? For those few moments, we won't be thinking about ourselves. We won't be thinking about our hair or our weight. We won't be angling to get attention or worrying about measuring up. We will forget about our precious selves, and focus on our precious God. We will be under a freer sky.

These moments of self-forgetfulness and deliberate meditation upon God will, with practice, turn into hours and days of seeking and worshiping our Savior instead of seeking our own glory. When we behold the beauty of the Lord, our Savior becomes larger and we become smaller—and so do our struggles with beauty.

John Piper puts it this way:

> Excessive preoccupation with figure and hair and complexion is a sign that self, not God, has moved to the center. With God at the center—like the "sun," satisfying a woman's longings for beauty and greatness and truth and love—all the "planets" of food and dress and exercise and cosmetics and posture and countenance will stay in their proper orbit.[9]

A Delightful Irony

For April and Eva—and for you and me—the gospel offers freedom from self-focus and vanity so that we may gaze and glory in our Savior's beauty all the days of our lives.

Then something totally unexpected happens. God's Word tells us that as we praise the beauty of our God, we will actually receive praise! It is one of the delightful ironies of Scripture: "Charm is deceitful, and beauty is vain, but *a woman who fears the LORD is to be praised*" (Prov. 31:30).

We've read this verse so many times that we hardly notice the second half; but there it is, in the black and white of God's unerring Word. The self-focused woman who spends her life chasing after charm and beauty will end up deceived and empty-handed. But the ex–glory robber, the God-glorifying, God-fearing woman will win praise for the beauty of her character.

Seek glory for your own beauty, and get nothing. Praise God's beauty, and get praise. What astonishing grace!

A godly woman, in and of herself, is not worthy of praise, but as she praises God she will be transformed. Others will notice and sing her praises, giving glory to God for his grace displayed in her life.

Let us all seek to be known and praised as women who praise and prize the beauty of God.

Not to us, O LORD, not to us, but to your name give glory. (Ps. 115:1)

Chapter Four

True Beauty
and Our Bodies

I doubt there is a woman alive who doesn't wish she could change something about her body.

That's certainly true for me. I have often lamented my knobby knees and complained about my thin, fine hair. I also dislike the appearance of my hands. I have very long fingers and veins that pop out no matter what I do.

I still remember being mortified one day in high school when a girl sitting next to me in orchestra class began scrutinizing my hands. She held up her small hand next to mine and announced: "Your fingers are *so* long."

And as if that weren't enough (still holding her hand up to mine), she then drew in the whole class. "Look everybody! Look at how much longer Carolyn's fingers are compared to mine." After that experience, my disdain for my hands only grew.[1]

What is it about your body that you don't prefer? If you're like me, you can rattle off at least a half dozen flaws without pausing for breath. Maybe you, too, have had someone point out your physical imperfections, perhaps in front of others, even. But we don't need their help, do we? We know exactly what we would change. We've discovered and examined, catalogued and complained about, observed and obsessed over every blemish, wrinkle, fat deposit, and flaw.

For many women, body image is a life-dominating issue, the source of much unhappiness and self-loathing. They can't imagine ever being satisfied with their body type or physical appearance.

"Many people struggle to accept themselves as they are," writes Jerry Bridges. "For them life is just a continuous adversity, not from outside circumstances, but from who they are."[2]

But we don't have to go through life struggling to accept our bodies. Scripture targets our body image issues and adversities, big and small, with liberating truth.

Hand-Crafted to Precise Specifications

At the foot of my bed lies a beautiful white and ecru yo-yo quilt. This is not just any quilt. It is the only thing in my house that I won't allow my grandchildren to jump or crawl on. And everyone in my family knows, if there's a fire and you have a chance to grab something—go for the quilt.

My mother made this quilt for me, entirely by hand. She used fabric that I picked out. She stitched and gathered each and every yo-yo. Her wrinkled hands laid them out in a pattern and then she sewed each one together until they formed a quilt. Since my mother has been with the Lord for several years now, this hand-made quilt is my most precious, tangible reminder of her life-long, attentive care.

And it is with attentive care that our Creator fashioned you and me. He created each of us, individually. He formed and molded us with *his* hands. "Your *hands* have made and fashioned me," the psalmist declares in Psalm 119:73. Job likewise proclaims: "Your *hands* shaped and made me" (10:8 NIV). What an amazing thought! Each of us, individually, is the *hand*iwork of the almighty, all-wise, infinitely creative God of the universe.

Not only did God fashion each of us by hand, he did so with intricate attention to detail:

> You clothed me with skin and flesh,
> > and knit me together with bones and sinews.
> > > (Job 10:11)

For you formed my inward parts;
> you knitted me together in my mother's womb.
> (Ps. 139:13)

Every part of our bodies was knit together by the hand of God. Our bones were carefully wrapped in muscle and tissue. He placed each blood vessel and layered our skin. The tightness of our curls and the jut of our jaws were meticulously defined. Our eyes and hair and skin were all painted to a perfect hue. He molded our ears and made our noses precisely prominent. He determined how tall our height, how long our limbs. He measured out the length of our toes and our fingers to their tips.

His hands did not slip; he did not make any mistakes. Right down to the thinness of our hair and the knobbiness of our knees, he created us, by hand, to be exactly who he wanted us to be.

All of our features—from our most prominent to the least obvious, from our favorite, to our least favorite—have been hand-fashioned by God himself.

Delight in His Flawless Design

While we may appreciate the fact that God has fashioned us by hand, there are implications to this truth as well. It means that when we fret about our flaws or complain about our imperfections, our argument isn't with the mirror or ourselves, it is with God. Jerry Bridges drives this point home:

> If I have difficulty accepting myself the way God made me, then I have a controversy with God. Obviously you and I need to change insofar as our sinful nature distorts that which God has made. Therefore, I do not say we need to accept ourselves as we are, but as God made us in our basic physical, mental, and emotional makeup.[3]

So when I complain about my hands, or sigh in disgust as I

blow-dry my thin hair each morning, I am arguing with God. I am telling the master craftsman that he has made a few mistakes and I could have done this creation thing a whole lot better.

We must not think lightly of perpetually grumbling about our physical appearance. Our dissatisfaction with our bodies is not harmless, nor is it a legitimate reason to feel sorry for ourselves.

If God made us with attentive care, by his own hands, we can trust in his wisdom and goodness. We can delight in his flawless design, whether or not it seems flawless to us. George MacDonald expounds on this truth:

> I would rather be what God chose to make me than the most glorious creature that I could think of; for to have been thought about, born in God's thought, and then made by God, is the dearest, grandest, and most precious thing in all thinking.[4]

We were born in God's thought, made by his hand. Let us resolve to accept our bodies with gratefulness to our Creator.

But as we've already learned, the truth about our creation is not intended to make much of us, but to make much of God. It is not to praise our own beauty or restore our deflated self-esteem, but to glorify our Creator: "Oh come, let us worship and bow down; let us kneel before the LORD, *our Maker!*" (Ps. 95:6).

When we mistakenly turn the spotlight of this glorious truth on ourselves and away from God, we may quote a verse like Psalm 139:14—"I am fearfully and wonderfully made"—and use it to make us feel better about our body image or give our friend's self-esteem a boost.

But in so doing, we forget the first half of this verse, and thus the whole point: "*I praise you*, for I am fearfully and wonderfully made" exults the psalmist. Instead of focusing on ourselves, we should lift our voices in thankfulness and praise.

Give God Your Heart ... and Your Body

Not only are we to be grateful for our bodies, we are answerable to God for every decision, big and small, about making our bodies beautiful. As Elisabeth Elliot once said: "We can't give our hearts to God and keep our bodies for ourselves."[5]

But what does God's Word say about beauty and our bodies? Does it tell me how to get my weight under control, or what my target weight should be anyway? Is it wrong to change my hair color? Wear a nose ring? Get breast implants?

God doesn't provide a list of which cosmetic procedures are allowable and which are not. Nowhere does he prescribe a daily time requirement for exercise or mandate a range for BMI. When it comes to beauty and our bodies, he doesn't give numbers and charts. And for that reason, neither will I.

I am not qualified to address various medical and ethical issues related to beauty and the body. Even if I were, there would be no way to cover them all or keep up with the latest options. And I will not bind anyone's conscience to my opinions. Rather, my goal is to remind us all that our consciences are accountable to the Word of God.

And God's Word doesn't come up short on this issue. It provides all the wisdom we need to understand how to reflect God's true beauty with our bodies. While body issues are often deep and sensitive, even confusing at times, Scripture is our unerring guide.

Diet Coke and Baby Carrots Take You Only So Far

"Please, please look at the topic of weight," begged Sadie. "In Christian circles, women still strive to be thin just like the world, and it is so hard as a young woman to know what is right. People say that it's okay to be weightier than what we see in movies and TV, but it doesn't seem as if anyone actually believes that."

What does God's Word say to Sadie? How should we think

about our weight? Is our goal to be thin, just not quite as thin as the cultural ideal? Sadie isn't sure if this is a godly objective, but she recognizes that we Christians often hold a double standard. While we would never tell someone they should be thin in order to be beautiful, we may believe that we should be, and strive for it all the same.

The simple answer to Sadie's question is that God does not make a worldly ideal of thinness a biblical goal. Friends, as much as we might hate to face up to it, the truth is, eating and exercising to achieve the cultural standard of a perfectly thin and toned body is not a godly pursuit. Try as hard as we may, we are not going to find any verse in the Bible that encourages it.

The biblical goal for our eating and exercising is clear: to bring glory to God. "So, whether you eat or drink, or whatever you do, do all to the glory of God," it says in 1 Corinthians 10:31.

Eating and exercising to glorify God require habits of self-control and discipline that contribute to the general health of our bodies. "Bodily training is of some value," Paul wrote to Timothy (1 Tim. 4:8). We are not to abuse our bodies, neglect our bodies, or overindulge our bodily appetites.

Medical advice and guidelines are gifts of common grace that can assist us in maintaining a healthy weight, and there are numerous resources that provide helpful eating plans and exercise routines. However, in this chapter, we want to focus on our motives for eating and exercise. Sadly, our eating and exercise habits often reveal a preoccupation with ourselves, rather than God's glory.

Take Catherine, for example. She says she is "an athlete at the collegiate level, surrounded by people consumed with their appearance and performance." She wonders about the role of exercising in the lives of Christians: "For me," she admits, "the more I exercise, the more I obsess about my body."

Similarly, one author records how thoughts about her eating circle in upon herself:

> I'm feeling fat and can't keep my mind off my weight. All day long, I think about food—avoiding food, eating certain kinds of foods, cooking diet dinners, feeling ashamed if I overeat, feeling great if I don't. Food has become my daily focus, even though I'm trying to lose weight with God's help and for His glory. I exercise, shop correctly, and snack on baby carrots. Every time we go out to eat, I ask the waitress or counter person about numbers of calories and fat grams, complaining about Diet Coke tasting like chemicals. While getting dressed in front of my husband, I point out my burgeoning waistline and inquire about his opinion of my wide behind. . . . I talk constantly about this struggle. . . . [6]

These two women describe a pattern we are all too familiar with: how quickly our exercising and eating leads to an obsession with how our bodies look, a preoccupation with our appearance. We try to be healthy—go to the gym and eat baby carrots—but the next thing we know, we can't keep our minds off our weight.

When our emotions become tied to whether we exercised today or stayed within our allotted calorie count, we have to consider what is motivating our eating and exercise routines. Do our thoughts run straight to how our eating and exercising (or lack thereof) will affect how we look?

If our diets and workouts become all about our appearance and how others view us, we are chasing self-glory, and not giving glory to God.

Never Diet the Same Way Again

So how *do* we stop exercising and eating for our own glory and glorify God instead? How do we appropriately care for our bodies without becoming obsessed with how we look?

We do it by pursuing a different goal: we must *steward our bodies for service to Christ.*

As Scripture instructs us in Romans 12:1: "I appeal to you therefore, brothers, by the mercies of God, to present your bodies as a living sacrifice, holy and acceptable to God, which is your spiritual worship."

In response to *the mercies of God*—which, if you will remember, Paul has spent the first eleven chapters of Romans elaborating on—we are to *present our bodies as living sacrifices.* This means that for Christians, all of life is devoted to the Lord's service, starting with willing obedience to God's commands, including our stewardship of our bodies. We are to eat and exercise in order to make our bodies effective and efficient in service to the Lord.

If we get this, we'll never go to the gym or on a diet in the same way again. As Christian women, we are not on a mission to be thin and have a perfect figure in order to be accepted by others. Rather, we are commissioned into the service of Christ. Our bodies are to be living sacrifices, *acceptable to God* (not other people), because they are dedicated to God's service.

Instead of getting on the treadmill or swimming laps to impress others, attract attention, and feel confident, we exercise to strengthen our bodies to carry out the tasks God has called us to do. We do not cut back on carbs or eat more fruits and vegetables because we are worried about how we look, but rather we maintain healthy eating habits so that our bodies may function at peak performance to serve God.

So, how do we know what is the "right" weight for us to be? Scripture reframes the question for us, and in so doing redirects our eating and exercise goals. The question should be: *How can I steward my body for service to Christ and not for self-glory?*

Stewarding our bodies for service is not an added burden or yet another reason to feel guilty about our eating and exercise habits. Rather, it frees us from the burden of striving for a cultural ideal for our own glory. When we are living for God's glory, because of his mercies, we are not enslaved by our own self-focus and sinful desires for attention and approval. We are free to focus on glorifying God and serving others and to "forget about our precious selves." This is freedom indeed.

Gracious Freedom for Disordered Eating

Any discussion of body and weight cannot ignore the precipitous rise of destructive eating behaviors such as anorexia and bulimia. As I noted in chapter 1, 65 percent of American women confess to disordered eating of some kind.[7] Courtney's harmful eating habits began at a young age:

> I began starving myself at age twelve, which progressed into bulimia within a few months. My body was changing and I longed to be beautiful, but I had a very skewed concept of beauty. In my mind beauty was thinness. After I started starving myself, thinness became what I lived for. I spent hours looking at *Vogue* and *Vanity Fair*, wishing I looked like someone else. I cared nothing about my health and only about my beauty.
>
> Everything I did revolved around my diet and exercise schedule. I avoided social situations and began losing friends because I didn't want to be questioned about my strange behaviors. I was obsessed, and although I was a healthy weight, I spent all my time trying to figure out how to get skinnier. I loved the control I thought I had to manipulate my body, to change my weight. I hated feeling full, and only felt "good" and "worthy" when I was empty.
>
> By the time I was thirteen, the eating disorder mindset had already taken hold. It ruled my life. I hated ingesting any food and tried my hardest to throw up after every meal. I did try to stop at multiple points, received counseling, and many times friends tried interventions with me, but I kept going back to it.
>
> I wound up in the hospital by age fifteen, wasting away. I was bleeding internally, in the early stages of heart and organ

failure, and according to my doctors, I had no chance of ever living a normal life again. My doctor told my mother that if I survived the next couple days, my body would be permanently impaired.

But my God is so much bigger. Prior to hospitalization, a sweet friend had been pleading with me and speaking the gospel to me regularly. I thought about what she said, but I didn't understand how God could love me enough to sacrifice his Son. In my most broken moment, alone in that hospital bed, God met me. I cried out to him, and he saved me: body, soul, and spirit.

My body miraculously healed in the coming months, following my release from the hospital. There is no other reason for my healing other than Jesus Christ himself. I'm still a sinner, and I still struggle in some body image related ways. Eleven years later however, it looks very different. By God's grace I am healthy and strong, and I am no longer living for thinness or beauty. My life is full of joy in Jesus Christ.

Today I try to plead with those who are struggling with eating disorders and help them identify the lies they believe. For example, Lie: It will make you beautiful. Truth: Your hair will fall out, your teeth will rot; you will look sick, anemic, exhausted, and void of life. I truly believe joy is the best cosmetic, and someone deep in an eating disorder experiences little to no joy. I also try to help them understand that God created them, and that they can be grateful for who he created them to be. All that, of course, second to telling them about the only one who can really save them, Jesus Christ.

Today, by the grace of God, Courtney works for a ministry that provides practical help and shares the gospel with troubled women. God healed her from the severe physical effects of anorexia and bulimia, and he rescued her from the lies and destructive eating behaviors.

While each woman's path to freedom from disordered eating may be different, God's grace is strong and sufficient to enable every person to resist every lie and reverse every destructive eating behavior.

A topic of this scope and seriousness is beyond the purview of this book, but may I plead with you?[8] If you are exhibiting a destructive eating behavior, please seek help, without delay, from a medical professional and a biblical counselor. As you read in Courtney's story, these behaviors have serious physical consequences and can lead to death.

But no sin or life-threatening situation is beyond the reach of God's grace, and he has provided doctors, pastors, and mature Christians to encourage women to resist temptation and receive hope, forgiveness, freedom, and grace to put away disordered eating. And if you are tempted to dabble or experiment with destructive eating, please do not fall prey to the Devil's lie that you can keep this under control or minimize its impact on your life, health, and spiritual well-being. As Courtney confessed, she, too, thought she was in control, but that was far from the truth (2 Pet. 2:19).

Please consider your motives for testing out dangerous eating behaviors: Are you, like Courtney, seeking to gain control over your body? Are you striving after a cultural ideal of beauty? Are you craving attention and glory for how you look instead of living to give glory to God?

Take a step of humility and confess your temptations to a trusted friend. Get help from a pastor and your doctor. Do not give temptation a foothold in your life (James 1:14–15).

May every woman who feels trapped in destructive eating behaviors or lured by this temptation remember that our Savior is the one who "breaks the power of canceled sin."[9] "For freedom Christ has set us free" (Gal. 5:1).

Humble Enhancement Is Not an Oxymoron

We have talked about how to *steward* our bodies for service to Christ and not self-glory. Now we will consider how we are to *enhance* the appearance of our bodies in a manner that reflects the beauty of God.

As I said at the beginning of this chapter, there is probably not a woman alive who doesn't want to change something about her appearance. Piercing and painting, tanning and tattooing, waxing and lasering, hair dyeing and relaxing, cosmetic procedures and surgeries—the list of alterations that we can make to our bodies today seems endless.

So where is the line, we all wonder, between what is acceptable and what is extreme? One thing every mother and teenage daughter knows for sure: if there is such a line, it changes with each generation.

But how should Christian women consider these issues? How do we reflect the true beauty of God? Making our bodies look better must be anchored in the truths we've already considered throughout this chapter: we've been created by God's hand and claimed for God's glory, therefore, we are accountable to God for what we do with our bodies. The gospel should inform every beauty-enhancing choice, whether it fades in six weeks or alters our appearance for a lifetime.

The gospel also helps us to be humble. It checks our criticism of other women's beauty choices by reminding us that we are all influenced by our sinful culture, we are all tempted to look good for our own glory, and we are all in need of a Savior.

Therefore, we must not insist that our opinions about piercing or tattooing are right and another woman's are wrong. We must not presume that we know the reasons why one woman chose to get cosmetic surgery or why another won't dye her hair. The gospel deflates our arrogant opinions and judgments and fills our hearts with humility toward others.

So how do we humbly develop biblical convictions that guide our choices on the entire spectrum of options for enhancing our appearance? Here are a few considerations.

Three Considerations

Consider Our Hearts. We know that we are to glorify God with our bodies and not wield them as tools for our own self-glory (1 Cor. 10:31). So does this mean that any effort to make ourselves beautiful, beyond the most basic grooming, is merely self-glorification? Of course not.

We remember from chapter 2 that God has given us a taste for beauty, a desire for beauty, and a propensity to make ourselves and the world around us beautiful. Scripture does not forbid women from making themselves beautiful. In fact, it says that women *should* adorn themselves, and tells them how to do it in a manner that glorifies God (1 Tim. 2:9–10; 1 Pet. 3:3–4).

But we must prayerfully consider our motives for whatever changes we want to make to our physical appearance, from the least to the greatest. We must ask ourselves: *Is my reason for _____ to bring glory to God or to impress others?* Or, to put it another way: *Would I be content and happy even if I did not receive compliments or attention for _____?*

If the measure of success for any beauty treatment is approval or attention from others, this is a red flag that we are pursuing self-glory and not God's glory.

Consider Safety. I recently read a news story entitled "Killer Eyelashes? Latest Beauty Craze Linked to Severe Allergies, Infections." It explained how many women, including a popular movie star, have experienced severe side effects from eyelash extensions and transplants. Problems range from conjunctivitis to allergic reactions causing extreme swelling, discharge, and discomfort.[10]

A report like this comes out on an almost weekly basis, and eyelash extensions are probably the least sensational. But it vividly illustrates the extreme measures women are willing to take in order to achieve a perfect face and body.

This story also highlights an important consideration for Christian women when it comes to enhancing our appearance. Not only is motive paramount, so is safety. Any effort to make our bodies lovely—which is not necessarily wrong—must also take into account our responsibility to keep our "fearfully and wonderfully made" bodies safe (Ps. 139:14). As Christian women, we must soberly evaluate the risks of various procedures or enhancements in light of the potential harm to our bodies.

Now for women whose normal appearance has been marred by accident or illness, or who have been born with a birth defect or disfigurement, cosmetic procedures and surgery can be a remarkable gift of God's common grace, healing and restoring a woman's appearance and dignity. The vast majority of us, however, must contend with the exploding popularity of purely elective cosmetic procedures that aim to change a woman's natural, God-given appearance.

For those of you who may have had cosmetic surgery in the past, you most likely chose this option based on the best medical and biblical information available to you at the time. But every woman must carefully consider the potential hazard to her body's health posed by an elective procedure or surgery. Remembering that our Creator has claim to our bodies, we must circle back around to the question of motive. *Why do I want this surgery or procedure so badly that I am willing to risk my health and safety?* The answer may reveal what we believe about beauty.

Consider Others. Choices about our bodies may be intensely personal, but they should not be made in isolation.

Thankfully, God has given us the church, a community of believers, with whom we share daily life. He has blessed us with older women to walk alongside us, help us discern our motives, and teach us—often from lessons hard learned—of the lies and emptiness of physical beauty. A godly husband will also lead his wife to prioritize true beauty as described in Scripture. And God has provided pastors to shepherd us and teach us to respond with biblical discernment to our culture's ungodly messages about beauty.

If we are considering a significant alteration to our appearance, we should seek godly counsel. No book or article can address each woman's unique situation, but mature friends can help us apply God's truth to our beauty decisions.

Teenagers, let me encourage you: God, in his infinite wisdom and kindness, has placed your beauty choices in the hands of your parents for the time being. You may not always agree with the limitations they impose, but you are called to obey, and that obedience is truly beautiful in God's eyes.

And moms, we are responsible to help our daughters understand our decisions from a biblical perspective. We must take as much time as necessary to explain our reasoning, making it easy for them to follow our lead, even when they don't fully agree.

One Simple Question

We've covered a lot in a few short pages, but we can sum it up with one simple question—a question we can ask before going to the gym or the salon: *Will this make me lovely and useful for the glory of God?*

This question isn't a magic pill, instantly dissolving our diet woes and our beauty desires. Rather, it is one simple tool to help us consider our decisions about our bodies, peel our eyes off ourselves, and take deliberate steps in the direction of God's glory rather than self-glory.

Some steps may be harder than others, and we will certainly fall and fail at times. But the gospel-centered woman remembers that the God who created her body also sent his Son, in the flesh, to save her from her sins (John 1:14). Because of his forgiveness, and by the power of the Holy Spirit, we can change. Life does not have to be a continuous adversity because of who we are. Instead, it can be a life of grateful worship to our Creator.

> So, whether you eat or drink, or whatever you do, do all to the glory of God. (1 Cor. 10:31)

Chapter Five

True Beauty and Our Clothes

"I used to be a young, pretty, artsy, hairstylist with lots of fun clothes," writes Monica:

> As a new believer attending a very conservative church, I was confronted in love about my clothing. I was covered completely and my clothes weren't too tight, but they were too "artsy" and would draw attention to me, and that was considered immodest. So, I settled on a safe wardrobe from Gap after a woman tried to re-dress me in Eddie Bauer attire, which clearly was not my style: I was twenty-one at that time, too young to wear Eddie Bauer and Ann Taylor clothing. I continued with this style for a few years. I didn't know who I was or what I liked anymore. I had conservative Christians telling me one thing and I had my worldly coworkers telling me another. I felt lost.

Monica didn't know what to do. She earnestly wanted to glorify God in how she dressed, but something about her fellow church member's advice didn't seem quite right. She was conflicted and confused.

How should a Christian woman think about being stylish and fashionable? Is there such a thing as too trendy and if so, how do we know what that is? How do we take care of our looks and yet avoid becoming obsessed with our appearance? How much time in front of the mirror is too much? Are there certain clothes or stores that God disapproves of? Is it even possible to know how to please God in the areas of clothes, cosmetics, accessories, and hair?

Like Monica, we may feel at a loss as to how to honor God with what we wear. And frankly, some of us are OK with that—we're a little afraid that if we learn what the Bible has to say, we'll have to overhaul our wardrobe. So we're fine being a little fuzzy on this topic.

Some of us are not interested for a different reason: we want to get back to studying God's beauty. Only shallow women want to talk endlessly about trivial women's issues like what we wear.

And then there are some of us who are quick to cry, "Legalism!" when it comes to any Christian discussion of clothing or appearance.

But God has clear, liberating, and life-changing words to say about what we wear. He speaks about our clothing in very specific terms, not once, but twice in the New Testament. Two different apostles, two different letters, two different recipients, and yet the message is the same.

In verses three and four of 1 Peter 3 it says:

> Do not let your adorning be external—the braiding of hair and the putting on of gold jewelry, or the clothing you wear—but let your adorning be the hidden person of the heart with the imperishable beauty of a gentle and quiet spirit, which in God's sight is very precious.

Paul makes a similar plea in 1 Timothy 2:8–10:

> I desire then . . . that women should adorn themselves in respectable apparel, with modesty and self-control, not with braided hair and gold or pearls or costly attire, but with what is proper for women who profess godliness—with good works.

Not only are these verses almost identical—braids and gold must have been all the rage in ancient Rome!—so is their context. If you examine the surrounding verses, you will see the wonderful backdrop to our wardrobe: the gospel. Peter and Paul remind their readers and us that the beautiful One, Jesus Christ, "himself bore our sins in his body on the tree" (1 Pet. 2:24) and "gave himself as a ransom for all" (1 Tim. 2:6).

The perfect God gave his perfect Son to redeem sinners like you and me. And it is his grace that causes us to "grow up into salvation" (1 Pet. 2:2), enables us to "die to sin and live to righteousness" (1 Pet. 2:24), and compels us to wear clothing that reflects the beauty of the gospel.

Monica was motivated by the gospel. Her life had been transformed by the good news of Jesus Christ. Her theology was sound, but she was lost when it came to practice. She had the *why*, but she needed the *how*.

Thankfully God's Word gives us both. Our Savior did not ransom us from our sins and awaken in us a desire to reflect his beauty, only to leave us with no clear pattern for how that looks. He drew it for us, right down to the plaits and the pearls.

A Fashion Faux Pas

The first thing we learn from these two passages is what Christian women are *not* to wear. Most of the time, we don't like to be told what *not* to do. In fact, being told not to do something is the very thing that often provokes us to do it in the first place.

Or if we do acquiesce, we may inwardly chafe at the imposition. Most irksome, perhaps, is when women (like Monica's friends from church) tell us what not to wear. That, we think, is getting a little too personal, going a little too far.

But we may appreciate such advice when it helps us avoid an embarrassing fashion mistake or improves our appearance. Take, for example, the TV show *What Not to Wear*, which at the time of writing this book is in its tenth season.

The cohosts comb through a guest's wardrobe and remove all of the fashion-offensive clothing. Then they outfit the person in more stylish, flattering clothes and present them in their new look to family and friends. In almost every case, the subject of the show appreciates their advice about what *not* to wear.

Scripture's "what not to wear" advice is the most valuable of all, because it tells us how to reflect the true beauty of God in our dress.

If we bristle at what we read in Scripture, our differences are not with well-meaning friends but with our Holy God. "The person who says, 'Jesus will not be Lord of my clothing' is little different from the person who says, 'Jesus will not be Lord of my money,'" writes Robert G. Spinney:

> Nor is it legalistic when God's people endeavor to obey God's instructions. D. Martyn Lloyd-Jones put it well when he said that if the "grace" we have received does not help us to keep God's laws, then we have not really received grace.
>
> To be sure, Christians can handle the subject of . . . clothing in a clumsy, unbiblical, and grace-denying fashion. That's a problem. But surely ignoring the subject is not the solution: by doing this, we imply there is no such thing as inappropriate clothing. God's people cannot afford to ignore this issue.[1]

Monica's Christian friends may have been clumsy in how they handled the subject of clothing. And no doubt you and I would have to admit we've also been clumsy at times. But God's grace enables us to rise above all that and discover how to wear clothing that honors the gospel. Scripture tells us what *not* to wear so that we can dress in a way that is truly beautiful.

Two Apostles, One Principle

Here is what 1 Peter 3 and 1 Timothy 2 tell us not to wear:

> Do not let your adorning be external—the braiding of hair and the putting on of gold jewelry, or the clothing you wear. (1 Pet. 3:3)

Women should adorn themselves . . . not with braided hair and gold or pearls or costly attire. (1 Tim. 2:9)

A superficial reading of these verses makes it appear as if Scripture is prohibiting braids and gold jewelry. We may wonder: *What is that all about?*

But with a closer look, we realize that this can't be true. In 1 Peter for example, if Peter is ruling out braids and jewelry, then he is also barring clothing, because "the clothing you wear" is on the short list of what our adorning should not be.

"Indeed, the Greek literally forbids the wearing of clothing at all," explains commentator Tom Schreiner. "Obviously Peter was not recommending that women wear nothing at all." Therefore we can conclude that "Peter did not prohibit women from wearing their hair nicely or from wearing any jewelry at all."[2]

So if he is not banning *all* braids and pearls and gold, what is he forbidding? Consider George Knight's comments on the 1 Timothy 2 passage: "It is the *excess and sensuality* that the items connote that Paul forbids, not braids, gold, pearls, or even costly garments in and of themselves."[3] The same can be said of Peter's instructions.

What Paul and Peter have in mind are the elaborate hairstyles worn by the ladies of the court and other wealthy women of the day:

> The sculpture and literature of the period make it clear that women often wore their hair in enormously elaborate arrangements with braids and curls interwoven, or piled high like towers and decorated with gems and/or gold and/or pearls. The courtesans wore their hair in numerous small pendant braids with gold droplets or pearls or gems every inch or so, making a shimmering screen of their locks.[4]

And so, as Knight summarizes for us: "The reason for Paul's prohibition of elaborate hair styles, ornate jewelry, and extremely expensive clothing becomes clear when one reads in the contemporary literature of *the inordinate time, expense, and effort* that elaborately braided hair and jewels demanded, not just as ostentatious display, but also as the mode of dress of courtesans and harlots."[5]

It was *excessive*: in time, expense, and effort. And it was *seductive*: women who dressed like this had a reputation for immoral behavior.

Not Excessive or Seductive

Styles have evolved dramatically through the centuries—no one will show up to your church this Sunday with an enormous tower of bejeweled braids on her head. Even if she did, it would hardly send the same message as in the first century. But it is not hard to see the relevance of these verses for us today. Excessive and seductive dress is more pervasive and outrageous than ever before.

The media pumps out a constant stream of images featuring the sensual attire of actresses, musicians, and models (the wealthy courtesans of our day). And while many of us can't afford to dress like the very wealthy, our modern economy makes it possible for us to spend excessive and inordinate amounts of time, money, and effort on our appearance. All of these messages and opportunities ceaselessly target our hearts, which are as susceptible as ever to the temptation to seek attention and glory through physical beauty.

The pressures we face when it comes to beauty are much greater than those of first-century women. And yet God's standard has not changed. He hasn't lowered the bar or exempted us from following these commands. Rather, in his perfect wisdom and love, God has provided truth in his Word that transcends time and change, and helps us navigate and rise above the cacophony of messages about beauty in our culture.

So what are we *not* to wear? We are not to wear clothing or jewelry that requires excessive time, money, and effort, or worse yet, are designed to seduce. But what constitutes excessive time, money, and effort? How much is too much?

As we have already learned, the woman who beholds God's beauty will find that matters of earthly beauty take their proper place. The woman transformed by the renewing of her mind will discern what is good and what is not (Rom. 12:2), what is excess and what is the right amount of time, money, and effort to spend on her looks.

What do we spend the most time thinking and talking about? What do we give the most money and effort to gain? Is it glorifying God's beauty or pursuing glory for our beauty?

Think about it another way: What would our friends or family say we are most enthralled with or captivated by? If the answer is clothing and cosmetics, then we may be guilty of excess, of wearing what God says *not* to wear.

Plaits and pearls turn out to be a lot more relevant than we may have thought at first.

What *to* Wear

Have you ever worn the wrong clothes to an event? I once heard the story of a woman who was invited to the White House for a function that she assumed was formal, only to find out that it was business casual and she was the only one wearing a gown.[6] How embarrassing.

No doubt we've all got stories like hers, although they probably didn't happen at the White House! But the most concerning wardrobe fail of all is when a Christian woman wears the wrong clothes.

Thankfully, we know the dress code. God has provided us with a very clear pattern for a Christian woman's dress. Not only has he told us what *not* to wear but he has also told us what we *should* wear. The apostle Paul sums up the Christian woman's style: "I desire then . . . that women should adorn themselves in *respectable apparel*, with *modesty* and *self-control*" (1 Tim. 2:8–9).

First, note the imperative: "women *should* adorn themselves." In warning against excess, Paul is not saying, "Forget about your appearance. A Christian woman shouldn't be concerned with how she looks." Quite the contrary—it matters a great deal what we look like. We are not to ignore our appearance; instead, we are to make a conscious effort to *adorn* ourselves, to look attractive.

The Christian woman does this by clothing herself "in respectable apparel." This doesn't harken back to your grandmother's dress code; rather, it means that we make a deliberate effort to wear clothing and accessories appropriate to the woman whose life has been transformed by the gospel. We take great care to dress in a way that honors the Savior.

What we wear should line up with, speak to, and be consistent with our profession of faith. Our dress should intentionally and carefully show our desire to reflect God's beauty in all things. And it should display the power of the gospel we have received to do just that. So just as we would choose a summer dress and not a ball gown for an afternoon picnic, so a Christian woman should only wear clothing that is appropriate to a gospel-centered life.

Modesty and Self Control

What are these respectable, gospel-glorifying clothes we are to wear? First Timothy 2:9 tells us: the dress code for a Christian woman is defined by the little phrase "with modesty and self-control."

Modesty and self-control are the heart attitudes that underlie gospel-appropriate apparel. But how do these attitudes determine what we wear? And what do they mean exactly? How do we know if we are being modest and self-controlled?

Modesty is a reverence for God and respect for others in our dress. It indicates a womanly reserve that shrinks from dressing in a way that may promote lustful thoughts. It even carries the idea of shame at contributing to temptation or dishonoring God with our dress.[7]

Self-control refers to the "feminine virtue" of restraint.[8] It means not dressing to excite passions in others or wearing clothing that "emboldens us to flaunt our sexuality."[9]

These qualities begin in heart attitudes before they end in wardrobe choices. To be modest and self-controlled means we dress from the inside out. "Any biblical discussion of modesty begins by addressing the heart, not the hemline," writes my husband:[10]

> There's an inseparable link between your heart and your clothes. Your clothes say something about your attitude. If they don't express a heart that is humble, that desires to please God, that longs to serve others, that's modest, that exercises self-control, then change must begin in the heart. For modesty is humility expressed in dress.[11]

But so often we ignore these essential heart attitudes and skip straight to the clothes, where we quibble and sometimes quarrel about how low is too low, how short is too short, how much is too much, how little is too little.

Modesty and self-control, when properly understood, settle the questions. The modest woman isn't a quibbling woman. She isn't flirting with immodesty or testing the limits of self-control. By very definition, modesty is a reticence, a hesitancy to get too close so as not to accidentally fall over into immodest dress. Modesty shrinks from doing anything that would tempt others.

"Every discussion of modest and immodest clothing at some point asks what could be called The Line Question," observes Robert G. Spinney:

> Where exactly is the line between acceptable and unacceptable clothing? How do I know where the line is? I won't cross the line, but could you please define precisely where the line exists? The word *modestly* addresses The Line Question because the modest Christians say, "I don't want to get near the line! I may not know *exactly* where the line is between acceptable and un-

acceptable clothing, but I know *approximately* where it is . . . and I will stay away from it."[12]

The modest woman is the woman who deliberately steps back from "the line" of immodesty. This does not mean she wears unattractive, unstylish clothing, but it does mean she's preoccupied with loving God and serving others rather than pushing the limits of immodesty.

Now where "the line" is may look different in different cultures and at different times. For example, showing one's ankles was considered immodest in Victorian times but is hardly an issue today. "The standards of modesty are somewhat (but not entirely) determined by cultural context," writes Spinney.[13] The point is that whatever culture she lives in, the modest woman seeks to serve those around her rather than test the limits of revealing or immodest clothing.

Preserving Purity

Modesty and self-control matter because a genuine love for God carries with it a corresponding hatred for sin, including the sin of lust. Immodest and seductive clothing can tempt men to lustful thoughts, and "a godly woman hates sin so much that she would avoid anything that would engender sin in anyone."[14]

"But if men lust, that's not my fault!" some may protest. While it is true that we are each accountable to God for our thoughts and actions, as Christians, we should feel a legitimate weight of responsibility to help protect and encourage godliness and purity in others (Luke 17:1–2). This isn't about pointing fingers and shifting blame. It is about honoring God and valuing the holiness of our brothers and sisters in Christ above our perceived "rights" to wear what we want.

While virtually all men are tempted by lust, godly men are attracted to godliness. Listen to what Seth, age twenty, has to say about modesty:

I grew up with two older sisters. They've taught me a lot about women. One of the things I've learned is there is a quiet and beautiful dignity about a woman who dresses conservatively. Any man would be fortunate to have a wife like my sisters, but what makes them really special is that they have too much self-respect and confidence to wear clothes that reveal too much. I use the word *confidence* because I feel a girl who's covered in all the right places is a girl who lives with the freedom of not having to rely on attention for her sense of self-worth. A girl with confidence is much more attractive to me than a girl who feels she has to exploit her body to receive attention or, worse, love.

My sisters are not ashamed of their bodies, and they wear the most current and stylish clothes. Yet they understand great men appreciate modesty. It doesn't matter how many girlfriends a man has had in his past, when he decides to settle down, his ideal wife will be one who lives modestly. A man who says he doesn't care about modesty or how his girlfriend dresses is lying.

When I marry, I want to find a woman I alone can fully appreciate. I believe young women should learn to value a sense of mystery. The more a woman destroys the mystery for a man, the more he will only be interested in what's going on from the neck down. All men are guilty of it, including myself, unfortunately. . . .

There's a saying that goes, "If you've got it, flaunt it." This is a lie. Instead, it should say, "If you've got it, protect it." Great women like my mother and sisters took this idea and lived their lives by it. This is the type of woman I'm interested in getting to know, because modesty and confidence in a woman is a very powerful and attractive combination.[15]

A modest girl is one "who lives with the freedom of not having to rely on attention for her sense of self-worth." The woman who is captivated by God's beauty and not chasing self-glory is *confidently* modest.

Of course, a woman may dress immodestly without realizing it, and new Christians in particular are often unaware of biblical teaching on this topic. We must never be harsh or judgmental about another woman's clothing. We must apply modesty first to our own hearts and wardrobes while being patient with others.

What does modest dress actually look like? While practical advice runs the risk of becoming outdated or perceived as extrabiblical rules, nevertheless it is helpful to have a tangible jumping-off place when considering how to express the attitudes of modesty and self-control in dress.

To this end, Nancy DeMoss offers two helpful guidelines. The modest woman refrains from "exposing intimate parts of the body" or "emphasizing private or alluring parts of the body."[16]

Take these two simple, practical thoughts into your closet, and they will go to work for you, helping you to be modest and self-controlled in your dress.

The Wardrobe of the Beautiful Woman

Modesty and self-control reflect the beauty of God's *holiness*. They point out the preciousness of his purity by prizing purity in our own lives and in the lives of our brothers and sisters in Christ. And by refusing to align ourselves with the provocatively sinful styles of the world, we reveal that we have been set apart for the service of Christ. We have been called to be holy as he is holy (1 Pet. 1:15–16).

Likewise, to display the beauty of God's *wisdom*, we must dress in a distinctly feminine manner. Our clothing and appearance must not leave someone wondering whether we are a man or a woman or whether we love being a woman. Our appearance should signal and celebrate the wisdom of God's beauty in creating male and female, in making them equal in worth and value, yet different in function and appearance.

Again, this will look different from culture to culture, age to age. My dad, for example, grew up in the early 1900s in a conservative Mennonite community. Although he eventually left the Mennonite church for doctrinal reasons, he retained many of their cultural ideals. As a result, he forbade my sisters and me from wearing pants at any time. In his culture only men wore pants. Needless to say, his daughters didn't always appreciate this restriction. But looking back, even though I disagree with his perspective, I am grateful he was eager for his daughters to dress femininely.

The issue is not skirts or pants (pants can be quite feminine in today's culture, and manly men in Scotland don kilts) or any other such distinction. The question is: in my cultural context, do my clothes celebrate femininity and the beauty of God?

It must also be said that as women we reflect the *loveliness* of Christ when we make ourselves look attractive and beautiful. Monica's friends were well-meaning but mistaken when they insisted that creative and artsy clothes were immodest. God's beauty does not stifle creativity in how we make ourselves beautiful. Rather, it provides gracious boundaries, which allow for a wide variety of tastes and styles.

When we enhance our appearance—modestly and with self-control, avoiding excess and sensuality—we reflect the loveliness of God. John Stott, in his comments on 1 Timothy 2:9, emphasizes this point:

> When a woman adorns herself, she is seeking to enhance her beauty. So Paul recognizes both that women are beautiful and that they should increase and exhibit their beauty. There is no biblical warrant in these verses for women to neglect their appearance, conceal their beauty or become dowdy and frumpish. The question is *how* they should adorn themselves.[17]

How should a woman dress? God's Word doesn't leave us conflicted and confused. It answers all our questions, and tells us ex-

Chapter Six

True Beauty and Our Trust

I grew up in the coastal town of Sarasota, Florida. After marrying and moving away, my husband C. J. and I returned often to visit my family. On one occasion, we were walking around St. Armand's Circle, a collection of shops and restaurants across the street from the beach, when we noticed a crowd gathering at a grove of palm trees in the center of the circle.

Curious, we went over to see what all the fuss was about, and discovered a model posing for a photo shoot. The photographer would take a few pictures, then back away while a half-dozen people swarmed in to touch up the model's makeup, fix her hair, adjust her clothes, and prod her into the perfect pose.

I might not look half-bad myself, if only I had a group of stylists who followed me everywhere! I thought. We watched for a few minutes and then kept walking, enjoying the shops and our iced coffees. But my mind kept wandering back to the model with her entourage.

It's true, maybe I wouldn't look "half-bad" if I had the wardrobe, and the lights, and the makeup artist, and the photographer, and the palm trees, not to mention the trainer and the chef and maybe even the surgeries. But I will never have any of those things. It is just me, my hair dryer, and my little bag of cosmetics.

But even if I did have the model's advantages, "not half-bad" is all I would look. To improve on that, I would have to have been born with the model's genetic makeup as well. The reality is, no matter how much you poke and prod and light me up, I will never achieve our culture's standard of perfect beauty.

The good news for me—and I'm guessing for a lot of you who don't look like models, either—is that God's Word offers a way for us to be beautiful. It is available to every woman, regardless of her age, her size, or any of her physical features. The woman who follows God's regimen for beauty will become genuinely beautiful.

This beauty is not for the select few, the elite, or the world-class. It is attainable by every woman who has repented and put her trust in Jesus Christ. Even so, it is not common or cheap, and many do not seek it eagerly. It is hard won, forged in trouble. But once gained, it never fades. It only grows more beautiful. It is the beauty that is most beautiful to our beautiful God.

A Godly Woman's Beauty Regimen

In the last chapter we looked at what 1 Peter 3 had to say about a Christian woman's clothes. But there is more. Peter goes on to give instructions for how a woman can make herself truly beautiful:

> Do not let your adorning be external—the braiding of hair and the putting on of gold jewelry, or the clothing you wear— but let your adorning be the hidden person of the heart with the imperishable beauty of a gentle and quiet spirit, which in God's sight is very precious. (1 Pet. 3:3–4)

We are to *adorn the hidden person of the heart with the imperishable beauty of a gentle and quiet spirit.*

Our *hidden* person is our inner person, our "true self."[1] And it is our hidden person we are to adorn—to clothe—with the *imperishable* beauty of a gentle and quiet spirit. Unlike clothes and jewelry that adorn our body, this imperishable beauty doesn't fade or fray. Once put on, it lasts forever.

If you're worried you'll have to shed your spunky personality in order to don this imperishable beauty, don't be. A gentle and quiet spirit is not a personality trait. It is the quality of a woman who meets adversity—slander, sickness, rejection, and loss—with a calm confidence in God.

A *gentle* woman is a woman of remarkable strength and tenacity, because she does not attack back when someone sins against her. Rather, she waits on God. Knowing that God is just, she can suffer without bitterness.[2]

To be *quiet* doesn't mean not to speak—although sometimes that might be a good idea—but it is "the sense of being calm, peaceful, and tranquil as opposed to restless, rebellious, disturbed, or insubordinate."[3]

If we were to sum up all that is meant by "a gentle and quiet spirit" in a single word, it would simply be: *trust*. This is the first step of a godly woman's True Beauty Regimen: trust God.

The women Peter was writing to needed to trust God. They were suffering trials of various kinds. Some endured "verbal abuse and discrimination" from a society scornful of Christianity.[4] Others longed for their unbelieving husbands to share their joy in Christ. Surely all of them were confronted with temptations related to beauty, such as how they dressed and wore their hair. Peter encouraged them with a grace-filled promise: you will become truly beautiful as you learn to trust in God.

God is trustworthy, Peter reminded the women. He deserves your trust in the midst of your trials, because "he himself bore our sins in his body on the tree" (1 Pet. 2:24). He has "suffered for you" (1 Pet. 2:21), enduring the agony of the cross on your behalf, so there is no situation or difficulty for which you cannot trust his love.

We too will grow beautiful as we learn to trust God in all our trials and temptations. In this chapter we're going to consider trusting God specifically in beauty-related adversities, since beauty, after all, is what this book is about.

Trust God When You Are Sinned Against

Our beauty-obsessed culture is a greenhouse for beauty-related unkindness and discrimination. These conditions spawn many trials for women. Few pains are as acute as being mistreated for our looks. Our appearance is so intertwined with who we are that any critique pierces the most tender part of us. It feels so unjust because it is unjust.

Perhaps we have experienced rejection because of how we look. At school, we aren't popular, included, or invited. Or maybe in the workplace we've felt demoralized as the more attractive girls get the promotions, even though we are more qualified.

We may harbor painful memories of being made fun of, scornfully criticized to our face or behind our back. Maybe your family puts pressure on you to be beautiful, and you feel like you never measure up.

Or perhaps your husband has been looking at pornography. This doesn't mean you aren't attractive to him, but it can feel, as one woman described it, "like a personal attack on my beauty." Most grievous of all, maybe your husband has committed adultery or left you for a younger, prettier woman.

The examples are many, ranging from mildly embarrassing to utterly devastating.

As women, we may eagerly embrace God's truth about beauty, but we still live in the real world, don't we? Sometimes it feels like no matter how hard we try to honor God with our bodies, dress modestly, and gaze upon God's beauty, instead of being honored and encouraged, we feel trampled on by others, even by other Christians.

These situations may tempt us to bitterness or even to attack back, both of which are the opposite of a gentle and quiet spirit. But God calls us to trust him even as we experience unjust suffering because of our appearance. He sent his Son to bear our sins and he shows us how to rise above mistreatment:

Christ also suffered for you, leaving you an example, so that you might follow in his steps. He committed no sin, neither was deceit found in his mouth. When he was reviled, he did not revile in return; when he suffered, he did not threaten, but continued entrusting himself to him who judges justly. (1 Pet. 2:21–23)

The secret to becoming more beautiful in trial is to *entrust ourselves to him who judges justly*. While people may be unjust, God is not. "Do you believe?" asks John Piper.

Do you trust, that God sees every wrong done to you, that he knows every hurt, that he assesses motives and circumstances with perfect accuracy, that he is impeccably righteous and takes no bribes, and that he will settle all accounts with perfect justice? This is what it means to be "conscious of God" in the midst of unjust pain.[5]

By looking beyond the injustices done to us and fixing our gaze on the perfect justice of God, we can endure unkindness about our looks without reviling in return. But this is not "merely a rule to be followed," adds Piper. "It's a miracle to be experienced. A grace to be received. It's a promise to be believed."[6]

Not only does God see and take note of every mistreatment, he also sees our obedience to him. Nothing slips his notice or his memory. Even when we don't see wrongs righted or our godly efforts rewarded in the time frame that we expect, or to the degree that we had hoped, we can trust that God will judge justly. It can be hard—even excruciating at times—to wait patiently for that justice to be worked out, but Christ has set the example for us. When we follow in his steps, we can resist the temptation to become bitter or to retaliate. We can, as our Savior did, continue entrusting ourselves to God.*

The woman who looks to God in the face of unkindness becomes

---

* If you are in a verbally or emotionally abusive relationship, let me encourage you to seek the advice of a pastor or godly friend in your church. And if you are being physically abused, you need to get immediate help from proper authorities.

more beautiful through suffering. Her face does not bear the lines of bitterness and a disturbed countenance. She displays a rare and remarkable beauty because she has learned to wait upon God. Her happiness is out of reach of those who have wronged her.[7]

Trust God When You Look at Others

Even when our looks aren't a trial *per se*, we are all tempted to compare ourselves to other women. We see them when we walk into a room or stroll through a crowd: the women who are prettier than we are. They are everywhere, aren't they?

Women have special powers of observation that enable us to instantly spot a woman with a prettier face, a skinnier figure, cuter clothes, or more of a flair for style than we have. We tend to rank everyone we meet on our own private beauty scale—placing them somewhere above or below ourselves.

Nothing ruffles a gentle and quiet spirit faster than comparing ourselves to other women. This can quickly turn into complaining. *I wish I had a gorgeous head of hair like hers. I wish I were as skinny as she is. She always wears such attractive clothes. I wish I could afford to dress like that. If only I were tall like her. If only I had her pretty face.*

Obsessive comparing and complaining lead to envy. Envy, as we know, makes us bitterly unhappy rather than gentle and quiet. It is an adversity, but in this case an adversity of our own making, with self-glory at the root. Why are we so unhappy that we don't have so-and-so's figure or that other girl's face? It is most likely because we want the attention she receives for ourselves.

Here again we must repent and choose to trust God. We must recall that it is our beautiful God who has decided what we look like *and* what every other woman looks like too. When we remember that he has ordained our beauty "lot" we can receive it as truly pleasant (Ps. 16:5–6). We can cease stressing, striving, and comparing.

In 1 Peter, God teaches us to trust him by giving us a different group of women to look at. Instead of picking out the prettiest girls in the room and marking them for resentment, we are to look to the godliest women:

> For this is how the holy women who hoped in God used to adorn themselves, by submitting to their own husbands, as Sarah obeyed Abraham, calling him lord. And you are her children, if you do good and do not fear anything that is frightening. (1 Pet. 3:5–6)

These are the heroines, the company of holy women of the past who trusted in God. Instead of comparing our physical appearance to other women, we should be measuring our hidden beauty next to these women, and striving to be like them.

Here's the good news: while most of us will never be the prettiest girl in the room, we can, by the grace of God, become like these holy women. When we cast off comparison and clothe ourselves with a gentle and quiet spirit, we can become beautiful children of Sarah.

Trust God for Your Husband

I had just finished speaking to a group of women on true beauty, when a woman approached me and commented: "That's all fine and good, God's perspective on beauty. And I believe it is true. But the reality is, that's not the message my husband receives from our culture about beauty."

She was worried. As she was getting older, her physical beauty was fading. But it troubled her that her husband, like every other man in our society, was constantly bombarded with images idealizing youth and physical beauty. Not to mention that her husband wasn't at the women's meeting to hear a message on biblical beauty. It's not that he had given her any reason to worry; she just appraised the situation and thought it sufficient cause for concern.

Ours is a culture that unfairly holds women to an ideal standard of physical beauty. Since it is a kind of beauty most of us will never attain, and will certainly never be able to maintain, we may worry about how we are going to hold onto our husbands' affection and attraction.

This is a recurring concern I hear as I interact with women about beauty. They wonder if they are still as beautiful to their husbands as their bodies change after childbirth and as they grow older. Even if their husbands attempt to reassure them, some women continue to worry. "I have a problem with accepting that my husband finds me as beautiful as he says he does," admits Stephanie.

This fear, along with our refusal to believe our husbands when they tell us we are beautiful, can cause tension in a marriage. "I struggle with the fear I'm getting fat all the time. It drives my husband crazy," writes Briana. Jen says the same: "I don't understand why I cannot trust my husband when he tells me how beautiful I am! It's so annoying to him when I say, 'You have to say that.'"

Friends, if there is one thing that frustrates a man, it is a wife who won't believe him on this point. Men don't like to feel as if they can never say or do enough to convince us that they appreciate our beauty. We do our marriages a disservice when we judge our husbands by failing to take them at their word.

But how do we deal with this fear that plagues so many of us? We must trust God for our husbands.

Some time ago, our husbands said, "Will you?" and we said, "Yes!" But it is God who brings a man and a woman together in marriage. He put affection in our husbands' hearts for us, and he has a good plan for our marriages. This is not to say that we won't face challenges, even severely painful ones. But no matter what trials we meet in our marriages, God will work them for our good and his glory (Rom. 8:28).

God is not distant from our marriages. He did not set them in motion only to leave them to run on their own. He is "a very present help" in marriage trouble (Ps. 46:1): present to care, strengthen, and comfort us, no matter our difficulties, big or small.

Confidence in God's personal involvement and tender care frees us from fear. Our hope is not in our husbands or in our beauty, but in the character of God, the constancy of his affections, and the surety of his purposes.

Here's where it gets amazing: The more we trust God, the more attractive we become. A gentle and quiet spirit adorns the whole woman, making her beautiful from the inside out. Her lack of anxiety, restlessness, and neediness, her carefree confidence in God's goodness makes her more lovely as the years go by. It is a beauty so profound, it can even attract unbelieving husbands to the gospel; they can be "won without a word" by the beauty of a wife's godly character (1 Pet. 3:1–2).

Does the significance of a wife's inner beauty mean she should not focus on her outward appearance? Tara confesses to some confusion:

> One thought that has often plagued me, and that I frequently use as an excuse for vanity and concern about appearances, is that my husband spends all day working with beautiful young women who strive to fit the culture's idea of beauty. Now, I don't fear for our marriage, but there is a part of me that feels some need to compete with these women. Is this a legitimate reason to pursue physical beauty? And if so, where do I draw the line?

Once again, trust in God puts physical beauty in its proper place. We don't strive to be beautiful to compete with other women, because God, and not our beauty, is the source of our hope for our marriages.

However, we should maintain our appearance, to the best of our ability, in order to serve our husbands. When we take care of our looks for our husbands, it blesses them and brings them pleasure and delight. It also honors them publicly. A wife who maintains her appearance tells the world that her husband is worth looking her best for. This tangible expression of honor is a great encouragement to our husbands. Genuine trust in God frees us from anxiety so that we can bless our husbands with our beauty.

Trust God in Your Singleness

For single women, the struggle with beauty may revolve around relating to single men and their expectations of beauty. As one girl put it:

> Even in the church, the godliest guys always go for the prettiest girls, leaving those of us who are "plain Janes" to watch from the sidelines. I believe inner beauty is most important, but guys seem to value outer beauty first and see inner beauty as no more than an added bonus.

All of us, men and women, are affected by a world that idealizes youth and physical beauty. In such a world, it can feel as if our looks dictate our destiny. But that is not true. It is God who sovereignly rules over all men and women. He has determined our looks and our marital status.

We must shift our focus by fixing our trust not on our appearance or men's expectations of beauty, but on God who directs our lives. Physical beauty does not have the last word and neither does a man's ideal of beauty. God's will determines all. Here's how Jonathan Edwards explained it:

> Love to God disposes men to see his hand in everything; to own him as the governor of the world, and the director of providence; and to acknowledge his disposal in everything that takes place. And the fact, that the hand of God is a great deal more concerned in all that happens to us than the treatment of men is, should lead us, in a great measure, not to think of things as from men, but to have respect to them chiefly as from God—as

ordered by his love and wisdom, even when their immediate source may be the malice or heedlessness of a fellow-man. And if we indeed consider and feel that they are from the hand of God, then we shall be disposed meekly to receive and quietly to submit to them, and to own that the greatest injuries received from men are justly and even kindly ordered of God, and so be far from any ruffle or tumult of mind on account of them.[8]

To "be far from any ruffle or tumult of mind" is Jonathan Edwards's eighteenth-century way of describing a gentle and quiet spirit. It is to trust in God's love and wisdom. It is to believe that his faithfulness (not forgetfulness) has planned our life's course. It is to choose not to grow bitter or discouraged. God knows how to arrange every relationship for the good of those involved and for his glory.

My good friend Dawn understands the temptation to grow bitter. At the age of forty-three, she was still single. She had honored God, walked in purity, and served in the church. She desperately wanted to be married, and yet God had not brought her a husband:

> I remember when I realized that the older I got, the more bitter I got, and the more bitter I got, well, that's not very attractive. I realized that the Savior needed to be my main focus as I was waiting, and so I started to pray for joy. My personality is very outgoing and talkative but that didn't mean I was joyful. I was not. I was growing very bitter, very stuck in my ways. So I prayed, *Lord, change me. I want to be a joyful woman.* I also prayed that God would do a miracle and bring my husband to my church.
>
> I always sat in the same seat at church. It was an auditorium that could hold several thousand people and my seat was near the back, in the middle of a row. One day I arrived at church only to find a man sitting there, in my seat. I sat down in the same row, with only one seat between us. His name was Arnie, and he started up a conversation with me. He was new to the

area, but obviously a Christian. We discovered that we had similar backgrounds. I could tell that he had a sense of humor. Under my breath, I prayed, *O Lord, please let me get to know this guy.*

That was right before Thanksgiving. Then all of December and January went by, and I didn't see Arnie, except for one brief moment. I looked every Sunday, but I couldn't find him. Only later did I learn that he was looking for me, too. During this time, God did another great work in my life. He was teaching me to trust him to bring my husband in his timing.

Then, at the beginning of February, I saw him again. We had a great conversation, and I learned that he was joining my church. He got my number and called me the next day. Things moved quickly from there. At ages forty-three and forty-two, you don't take your time. I learned that, like me, he had never been married. He got to know many of my friends, and they all really liked him. After a wonderful and whirlwind courtship, Arnie and I were married in July of that year. I had prayed that God would bring my husband to my church. Not only did he answer that prayer, he brought him to my very seat.

As I look back now, forty-three years of waiting was extremely hard. But my biggest regret is how often I charged God for not being good, when, in fact, he really did have the best plan in mind. Praise God he didn't listen to my complaining and didn't give into my whining and instead chose what was best for me. It was as if he said: I am not going to treat you as your sins deserve and I am going to bring you the perfect man for you and you are going to understand what the love of a husband is. Today, I would not change a single thing about his plan. What we have in this marriage is so much better than anything I would ever have imagined.

To see Dawn and Arnie together is to smile. They have a sweet and wonderful marriage. But, you know what? To see Dawn *before* Arnie was to smile, too. As she chose to trust God and repent from bitterness, she became joyful and lovely. In fact, the first thing Arnie noticed about Dawn was her joy—her smile, her laughter, how easy she was to talk to, and how much fun she was to be with. Arnie saw Dawn's true beauty.

Not every woman who desires marriage and trusts God for marriage will get married. But as we look to God and as we study his Word, we begin to learn that even those things he withholds from us are for our good (Ps. 84:11). As Elisabeth Elliot so beautifully expresses it: "God never denies us our heart's desire except to give us something better."[9]

Trust God as You Age

If you are a young woman, you may not think you have to worry about aging yet. If you've even thought about it, it seems a long way off. You'll deal with it when you get there. But how we pursue beauty today has everything to do with how we age. If we live long enough, we will all have to trust God for aging. And if we have trusted God all along, we will grow more beautiful as we age.

In today's culture, youth equals beauty. This means that one day, we will all fall short of the standard. Sure, we can try to forestall the effects of aging and fake the appearance of youth with creams and tucks and lifts, but Paul's description of aging is as blunt as it is inevitable: "Our outer self is wasting away" (2 Cor. 4:16).

Aging pries loose the fingers that have so tightly grasped onto the physical beauty of youth, one by one. The aging woman no longer relies on her looks for happiness or friendship. She can't bank on her figure to get or keep a husband. She isn't striving to gain beauty, and she has stopped worrying about keeping it. While she doesn't look as outwardly attractive as she once did, it doesn't matter like it once did.

God's Word doesn't deny or mask the effects of aging (as do so many of our beauty treatments). Instead, it declares that growing old in God is a gift, a blessing. And, if we have been applying the godly woman's True Beauty Regimen all our lives, it is a remarkable, grace-empowered achievement of truly stunning beauty.

Scripture looks at aging from the perspective of the finish line and rejoices with each milestone of maturity: congratulations, you are getting closer! From this direction, even the outward, physical signs of aging are seen in a different light: "Gray hair is a crown of glory; it is gained in a righteous life" (Prov. 16:31). God's Word celebrates aging, and we should celebrate it, too. For every day brings us closer to the day when Jesus Christ "will transform our lowly body to be like his glorious body" (Phil. 3:21). Even though our physical beauty will inevitably fade, we have the hope of the resurrection, where he will change our lowly body to be like his glorious one. We will don a beauty beyond anything that we can imagine.

Though many women become hard and bitter as they grow old, a woman who trusts God, who pursues a gentle and quiet spirit through the many trials and temptations in her life, grows more radiant and lovely, even as she wastes away. Her beauty is an *imperishable* beauty, after all. This is the powerful, living paradox of true beauty.

Trust God in Whatever You Fear

Responding to trials with the gentle and quiet spirit of trust in God makes us truly beautiful:

> For this is how the holy women who hoped in God used to adorn themselves, by submitting to their own husbands, as Sarah obeyed Abraham, calling him lord. And you are her children, if you do good and do not fear anything that is frightening. (1 Pet. 3:5–6)

The holy women of the past adorned themselves with trust in God. By submitting to their husbands (a topic that requires a book all its own!), they trusted in God for their life and became beautiful.

We are Sarah's daughters, inheritors of her legacy, if we *do good* (the second part of our True Beauty Regimen, which we'll address shortly) and *do not fear* that which is frightening.

We've talked about many frightening things in this chapter: sinful husbands, extended singleness, receiving unkindness through the derision of others, and losing attractiveness through the deterioration of aging.

Scripture doesn't deny that these are frightening possibilities. And yet we are not to fear. We are to trust God, for he is trustworthy. He holds all frightening things in his hands, directing them with absolute sovereignty, infinite wisdom, and lavish love.

When we wake up each morning and choose not to fear the frightening things in our day or in our distant future but trust God, we are applying the godly woman's True Beauty Regimen.

If we adorn ourselves with a gentle and quiet spirit by responding to trials, temptations, loss, and fear with an unshakeable trust in God, we will achieve a rare and real beauty.

This beauty is "very precious" in the sight of God. The phrase means "costly," and it is set in sharp contrast to the costliness of the immodest woman's extravagant adornment.[10]

Our trust in God truly costs something, and it is truly worth something. The temporal cost of trusting God is eternally valuable. It shows forth the worth and loveliness of the gospel. It demonstrates the power, trustworthiness, and beauty of God in Jesus Christ because it is only his power at work in our hearts that makes such seemingly impossible trust possible.

> Let your adorning be the hidden person of the heart with the imperishable beauty of a gentle and quiet spirit, which in God's sight is very precious. (1 Pet. 3:4)

Chapter Seven

True Beauty and Our Works

Women have been flirting with danger in their daily beauty routines for millennia. The ancient Egyptians, Persians, and Romans, for example, used antimony sulfide drops as eye glitter, eventually drying up their tear ducts and destroying their vision. Little better were the eye drops of the sixteenth and seventeenth centuries, made from the poisonous herb belladonna and used to achieve a dewy look. They eventually caused glaucoma.[1]

In the nineteenth century, many tried to achieve a naturally porcelain look by swallowing a potion of vinegar, chalk, and arsenic—poisonous, even in small doses. The application of lead and vinegar to the face, previously employed by Elizabethan women to achieve the same effect was, needless to say, only marginally safer.[2]

More recently, women applied a precursor to mascara known as Lash Lure, which was not only a permanent dye, but also proved to be toxic, blinding, and potentially deadly. So hazardous, it was at least partly responsible for Congress passing the 1938 Food, Drug, and Cosmetic Act, allowing the FDA to regulate cosmetics.[3]

Even when they weren't dangerous, daily beauty regimens of the past could be painful. Imagine plucking your hairline to achieve the ideal high forehead as Renaissance women did. Or wearing a corset, which often required one servant to hold you down with her foot while the other pulled your waist to an agonizing eighteen inches.[4]

Thankfully for the average woman today, our daily beauty routine is not as dangerous or painful. But through the many changes in fashion and in safety, one thing stays the same: we all have a daily beauty regimen. When we wake up each morning, we all do something to enhance our appearance—or at least minimize the damage from a night of sleep (or lack thereof). We take a shower, brush our hair and our teeth, smear concealer on the bags under our eyes, maybe apply some lip gloss or mascara. Some of us may do much more, others a little less. But we all do something.

As we discovered in the last chapter, there is a beauty routine that exceeds all others in making us truly beautiful. It is the godly woman's beauty regimen. It has proven to be 100 percent effective, and while it is costly, it is precious in God's sight.

Our True Beauty Regimen begins with trust in God. The second step is found in 1 Timothy 2:9–10:

> Women should adorn themselves in respectable apparel, with modesty and self-control, not with braided hair and gold or pearls or costly attire, but with what is proper for women who profess godliness—with good works.

Here is the second part of the most unique, most effective beauty regimen ever prescribed. Apply trust in God, *with good works*, and you will not fail to become genuinely beautiful.

A Public Service Announcement

What are good works, exactly? Jerry Bridges calls them "deliberate deeds that are helpful to others."[5] They are tangible acts of kindness that serve and bless. And good works are how we as women are to "adorn ourselves," to make ourselves beautiful.

But mention good works and some people get concerned: if we focus on good works, do we risk taking something away from the glory of the gospel?

Scripture says the opposite: good works bring glory to God and adorn the gospel.

"Let your light shine before others, so that they may see your good works and give glory to your Father who is in heaven," the

Savior instructed in the Sermon on the Mount (Matt. 5:16). Martyn Lloyd-Jones comments that when people see our good works: "They will ask, 'What is it? Why are these people so different in every way?' . . . And they will be driven to the only real explanation which is that we are the people of God, children of God. . . . We have become reflectors of Christ."[6]

Scripture emphasizes the importance of good works for all Christians, and for women in particular in 1 Peter 3:6, Titus 2:3–5, 1 Timothy 5:9–10, and Proverbs 31:31. This last passage ends with the exclamation, "Let her works praise her in the gates."

In fact, here in 1 Timothy 2:10, God tells us that good works are "proper for women who profess godliness." Robert Spinney explains that this phrase means:

> *To make a public announcement or to convey a message loudly.* Our lives make public announcements. The godly woman's public announcement must consist of good works, not questionable clothing. . . . The implication here is that both good works and improper clothing have a Godward element: one provokes men to praise God while the other encourages men to demean Him. . . . God's reputation is at stake in our public professions. God's glory is more clearly seen when we abound in good works, but it is obscured and misunderstood when we make public announcements with improper clothing.[7]

Good works done for the glory of God do not distract from the gospel or undermine the gospel—that is what immodest clothing does. Good works are essential to our gospel proclamation. They promote Christ's reputation, they bring glory to God, and they make us beautiful for the sake of the gospel.

To be gospel-centered in our good works means that we don't *rely* on those good works for our righteousness before God or our forgiveness from him. We are accepted before God only because of Christ's life, death, and resurrection. We are able to stand before God only because of the righteousness of Jesus Christ. We do good works because we have *received* forgiveness, not in order to *earn* forgiveness.

A Reputation for Good Works

To learn more about these good works that make us beautiful, we only need to turn the page from 1 Timothy 2 to 1 Timothy 5:9–10. Here Paul gives counsel to Timothy about widows, but in so doing, sets the standard for godly women by describing a lifestyle of self-sacrifice:

> Let a widow be enrolled if she is not less than sixty years of age, having been the wife of one husband, and having a reputation for good works: if she has brought up children, has shown hospitality, has washed the feet of the saints, has cared for the afflicted, and has devoted herself to every good work.

These good works don't comprise a checklist; they describe the godly woman's character. She has *a reputation for good works*. And her reputation is important to her because it speaks to the reputation of her God. She grasps the sobering fact that "God's reputation is at stake in [her] public profession" of godliness.[8] The beautiful woman desires to be known for good works because she longs for God's good work to be known.

Every Christian woman should strive to have a reputation for good works. There are no good works specialists. This is not for the gifted or enthusiastic few. We all must raise our hands to volunteer. All of us can do good works, for God has called all of us to do good works. And as Jerry Bridges puts it, good works are "deliberate." We don't fall into them or stumble upon them. We must choose to practice good works.

In 1 Timothy, the apostle Paul provides us five categories of good works. This list is not exhaustive, and it is not to be applied exhaustively. But if we want to become truly beautiful, we will make this list of good works an essential part of our daily beauty regimen. To get a picture of this woman of good works, we'll touch briefly on each example.

Five Good Works (Plus One)

"Brought Up Children." The heart's desire of a godly woman is to raise her children to honor and serve the Savior. To that end, a mother should give herself to bringing up her children "in the discipline and instruction of the Lord" (Eph. 6:4). A woman who doesn't bear children can be a godly influence on children in her church and community, and care for orphans.

This good work is difficult, obscure, and messy—whether you are raising your own children or caring for someone else's. You may not feel very beautiful as you change dirty diapers, wipe noses, and wash smelly laundry on three hours of sleep. But who is more beautiful to a child than the woman who cares for him or her? And bringing up children to serve the Lord is precious to our Savior, who said, "Let the little children come to me" (Matt. 19:14).

"Shown Hospitality." This is a home-based good work. To show hospitality means "meeting the needs of others through the use of one's resources, specifically in and through the context of the home."[9] The godly woman practices hospitality by having people into her home, giving refuge and refreshment, and by taking meals and resources from her home to others.

"The ultimate act of hospitality was when Jesus Christ died for sinners to make everyone who believes a member of the household of God," writes John Piper.[10] The hospitable woman desires to reflect the beauty of Christ's hospitality. Regardless of the size of her home or her budget, she wants to extend to others the unmerited love and grace that she first received from the Savior.

"Washed the Feet of the Saints." Foot washing was an essential but menial task in ancient times, as everyone's feet were either dusty or muddy from the roads. It was a chore usually reserved for household servants. So to wash the feet of the saints meant to be

a humble servant, to take on the tasks no one else wanted to do. In other words, the woman who wants to be beautiful is willing to take on the dirty jobs, the lowly jobs, and the unattractive jobs.

When we serve others, we follow the example of the woman who anointed Jesus's feet: "For she has done a beautiful thing to me," Jesus said in Matthew 26:10. And so he says to us when we humbly serve the saints.

"Cared for the Afflicted." The beautiful woman is like a nurse in a hospital, on call, ready to help the suffering—whether they are afflicted physically, mentally, or emotionally. To do this good work, we must draw near to that which is raw, ugly, difficult, and painful. In so doing we properly reflect our Savior's reputation as one who is "acquainted with grief" (Isa. 53:3), "near to the brokenhearted" (Ps. 34:18), "a very present help in trouble" (Ps. 46:1), and "who comforts us in all our affliction" (2 Cor. 1:4).

No doubt we can all think of women who have shared a Scripture, brought us a meal, or simply been there for us in our afflictions. Who, in the midst of grief or pain, is lovelier than a woman who cares? When we care for the afflicted, we extend God's care and comfort, and this is beautiful.

"Devoted to Every Good Work." If you had to describe her in a sentence, you would say that the godly woman "has at all times thrown her whole heart into good deeds."[11] As someone once said, you are to do all the good you can, by all the means you can, in all the ways you can, in all the places you can, at all the times you can, to all the people you can, as long as you can.

"Brings Good News." There is one more good work not mentioned specifically in 1 Timothy 5, but which is commanded of every Christian. We must all be faithful to share the good news of the gospel of Jesus Christ to a lost and dying world. Evangelism is, in one sense, a message about beauty. It is a message about beauty created, beauty lost, and beauty restored.

What greater good work can there be than to share the good

news of the beautiful gospel to those who are blinded to the beauty of God in Jesus Christ? "How beautiful upon the mountains are the feet of him who brings good news, who publishes peace, who brings good news of happiness, who publishes salvation" (Isa. 52:7).

This is the second step of our True Beauty Regimen: we are to deliberately throw ourselves into good works. As we trust God and do good works, we will be beautiful in the eyes of those we serve, and most of all, precious in the sight of God.

We All Strive for the Prize, But It Isn't a Competition

After considering these six categories, the True Beauty Regimen might seem harder than you thought at first. In our frenetic society, we are already so busy with homework, jobs, and families. Six more big items on the to-do list may seem like an overwhelming, not-so-attainable standard of beauty after all.

But we must remember that Paul was talking about what these widows had accomplished throughout their lifetimes, not all at once. Giving themselves wholeheartedly to good works no doubt looked different at various times in their lives.

Moms of small children apply this beauty regimen every day, all day. As my husband often says, no one has a harder job than a mom with young kids. This statement felt true to me when I had little ones, and now that I am watching my daughters mother their children, it rings truer than ever.

You may not be the first to show up in a crisis or do the most hospitality, but you are washing little feet all day as you humbly serve your family. I pray you know God's pleasure in your faithful service. It is beautiful to him, and even though no one else may see, "your Father who sees in secret will reward you" (Matt. 6:4).

I also know women who are eager to do good works, but despair because of limitations such as sickness, aging, a disability, or a crisis. If you feel "put on the shelf," as Charles Spurgeon vividly described it, then take his advice and pray for others.[12] For there is "no greater kindness" you can do for someone.[13] You may not be able to serve others in physically demanding ways, but you can still grow beautiful through good works.

We all have different capacities and gifts, and so we must resist the temptation to compare. This is not a beauty competition. Just as we should not compare physical beauty, we should not compare good works. Every woman who sincerely serves the Savior grows truly beautiful.

It all comes down to one question: Do I strive for a reputation of good works in order to reflect the Savior's good work? When all is said and done, after we have spent and been spent doing good works, we must make a heap of all our good works and lay them at the foot of the cross.

Saved, She Served; Tried, She Trusted

True beauty is one of those things you have to see in order to appreciate. So let me introduce to you my dear friend Kathy. She is a recent widow, and a woman with a reputation for good works and trust in God.

Kathy was saved and came to our church soon after college. She offered to babysit our girls, without accepting payment, and she quickly became like one of our family. My grown, married daughters still call her "Aunt Kathy."

She worked as a sign language interpreter for the hearing impaired and outside her job, she spent every spare moment serving others. Kathy cared for children, sang on the worship team, interpreted during the Sunday sermon, organized church events, made meals for people, took a single mom and her daughter into her home, even made numerous trips into downtown Washington, DC, to reach out to prostitutes. To say the least, Kathy threw herself into good works.

I remember how Kathy would return from some service project or outreach, and with her self-deprecating sense of humor tell me funny stories of mishaps, awkward moments, or downright scary situations. We'd laugh until tears ran down our cheeks.

But there were a few sad tears, too. While Kathy was busy doing good works, her friends were getting married. Year after year went by, and friend after friend got married, but God did not bring a husband for Kathy. And yet she filled those years with serving, and God gave her much joy as she continued to trust him.

When Kathy was thirty-four years old, God brought John into her life. He was obviously the perfect one for Kathy. John had a great sense of humor, and he was a talented musician. Their gifts and personalities complemented one another perfectly.

After they were married, John and Kathy wanted to start a family right away. But month after month went by, and Kathy was unable to get pregnant. Disappointment followed disappointment. The infertility treatments they tried were to no avail.

Once again, Kathy needed to trust God. After waiting for years to get married, now she wasn't able to have children. But her trust in God never wavered, and the Lord led her across the ocean to an orphanage in Romania where she and John adopted two small boys, Gabriel and Joseph. A few years later they adopted a little girl, Amanda.

As her children grew, Kathy's life and home was a hub of good works. She hosted dinner guests, out-of-town guests, and long-term guests in need of a place to stay. She served in the church's women's ministry. With her husband John, she also served in children's ministry, adoption ministry, music ministry, married couples' ministry, small group ministry, and evangelism ministry.

When someone had a crisis—a young boy dying of brain cancer, a husband and father with severe epilepsy—Kathy organized care and was often close by to help and support those who were suffering.

And when John and Kathy were no longer needed on the Sunday morning worship band, they got their teenagers together, formed a family band, and began to serve the children on Sunday mornings. As always, Kathy's whole life was devoted to good works for her family, her church, and those who needed to hear the gospel.

Then, a few years ago, John began to experience some muscle weakness in his arms and legs, and he began to have some difficulty walking and playing his guitar. Eventually, John saw a doctor and received the devastating diagnosis: ALS, otherwise known as Lou Gehrig's disease. This fatal illness would first rob him of his ability to work, then his ability to walk, and eventually his ability to care for himself.

Kathy cared for John and worked full time to support the family through his long illness. As she had cared for so many in the church who were afflicted, now she cared for her husband. John became progressively weaker in body, but he grew stronger in spirit day by day. His remarkable faith was a profound encouragement to all who knew him.

In January of 2011, John went home to be with the Lord. My friend Kathy, married at thirty-four, was now a widow at age fifty-eight. Her husband and best friend was gone.

It would be so easy for Kathy to lose trust in God, to charge him: *Haven't I faithfully trusted you all these years? Haven't I given my whole life to doing good works for your glory? This is not the way it was supposed to be!*

But Kathy doesn't charge God. She has not grown bitter or angry. Of course she grieves, and she has questions that will most likely remain unanswered this side of heaven. But even in the midst of her grief, Kathy chooses to trust God and serve others. In fact, this past year, Kathy left everything familiar, including life-long friends and a good job and moved with one of her sons and her daughter to help us start the church plant that my husband leads.

She greets on Sundays, reaches out to new folks, serves in children's ministry, hosts church gatherings at her home, and volunteers at a local ministry for women transitioning out of the adult entertainment industry. She does what she has always done her whole life: trust God and do good works.

Life is not always easy for Kathy. She misses John. She misses many dear friends. And so, she cries sometimes when I see her at church or when we get together for coffee. And then, in typical Kathy fashion, she laughs in the midst of her tears. Recently, I talked with Kathy at church. She told me how she was doing and we both cried a little. But then she took a deep breath, dried her eyes and described her afternoon plans.

She was going to spend time with several women who have transitioned out of the adult entertainment industry. They were going to make a cake and watch a movie together. That was all. But she wasn't going to sit at home and feel sorry for herself, not while there were women who needed a friend and who needed to hear the gospel.

That's what Kathy does. She cries. She trusts. She laughs. She does good works. And she grows more beautiful every day.

In one sense, Kathy is an ordinary woman like you and me. But seen in another light, through God's eyes, she is like the beautiful heroines of the past. She does not fear that which is frightening. She puts her hope in God. She trusts him and she does good works. She is a woman clothed with strength and dignity, who laughs at the days to come (Prov. 31:25).

She is a true beauty.

Each Day Brings Us One Step Closer to True Beauty

While women in our culture thirst after what few drops of glory and goodness they can drain from physical beauty, they look older even as they try to look younger, more hollow and hardened even as they chase after an elusive happiness.

By contrast, the woman who pursues the godly woman's True Beauty Regimen grows radiant as she looks to God in adversity

(Ps. 34:5). She lights up the faces of those she serves, and most precious of all, she pleases our Savior.

Christ is the beautiful One. His glory and splendor, his sacrifice and salvation, define true beauty. It is not the world that defines beauty. It is not the latest fashions, or a photoshopped image, or an ideal body type. True beauty is, to the world, as incomprehensible as it is undeniable.

"We are the people who know what beauty is," writes Albert Mohler.[14]

> Not that we have seen it yet with our eyes, but we have seen it in a foretaste, and we have been promised it with an assured promise. In this life, we live amidst the pretty, the corrupt, and the artificial. We live among those who do not believe beauty exists, and among those who think beauty can be manufactured. In such a context, we are the ones who have to say we know beauty, and it is none other than Jesus Christ the Lord.[15]

For the Christian woman, each day brings us one step closer to true beauty. As earthly beauty fades away, imperishable beauty grows stronger and lovelier, and the most beautiful vision we will ever see draws nearer—the day when we will "behold the king in his beauty" (Isa. 33:17), when we will see our beautiful Savior face-to-face.

Until that beautiful day, let us gaze upon the beauty of the Lord all the days of our lives, and pursue a beauty that is precious in his sight.

True beauty is to behold and reflect the beauty of God.

> And let the beauty of the LORD our God be upon us.
> (Ps. 90:17 NKJV)

Appendix:
True Beauty
and Our Children

How do we raise our children in this world of beauty gone bad?

Mothers can feel as if a worldly, distorted view of beauty has been ominously rising like a wave, only to crash on our heads just as we get our mothering feet wet.

The pressure on young girls to conform to an ideal of physical beauty is so much more intense today than it was a generation ago. The beguiling voice of the seductive woman is so much louder and more enticing to young men than it used to be.

We mothers can feel helpless in the face of this cultural tsunami. False messages about beauty saturate music and movies, are splashed on TVs and graphic T's, and soak through the whispers and status updates of kids from school.

How can we possibly lift our daughters above the rising tide of destructive messages about beauty from our culture? How can we hope to rescue our sons from the temptation to seek a false ideal of physical beauty?

Take heart, dear mothers. We may feel helpless, but God has promised to help us: "Fear not, for I am with you; be not dismayed, for I am your God; I will strengthen you, I will help you" (Isa. 41:10).

The beauty of grace that overwhelmed our own hearts through the gospel of Jesus Christ has lost none of its power. Our Savior can do for our children as he did for us. Grace makes true beauty irresistible. So we pray with hope in God to open the eyes of the hearts of our children to the dazzling beauty of Jesus Christ.

But our parental prayers, as we know, are meant to issue in faithful action. What biblical strategies can we employ to lead our children, in age-appropriate ways, to understand and embrace true beauty?

Here are a few suggestions which, when set in the sturdy framework of biblical parenting, can help us train our children to recognize, celebrate, and pursue true beauty.

Show Our Children True Beauty

Example is essential. We must not merely point at true beauty like a distant mountain peak; we must dwell with our children as a vibrant model of true beauty. Humanly speaking, no one will make a deeper impression on children than a truly beautiful mother. And yet we often underestimate the effect of our example.

Ask yourself: What am I teaching my children about beauty through my actions, words, priorities, and life?

Sadly, our children will absorb our self-absorption; they will vainly follow our vanity. If we are consumed with what others think about how we look, our daughters will learn that self-focus is the way to fulfillment. If we spend exorbitant time and money on our appearance, we are teaching our sons to prize physical beauty above all.

But if we spend our days gazing at the beauty of God, beholding him in his temple (Ps. 27:4), we will show our daughters how to find true joy and satisfaction. If we devote our lives to serving others, we will encourage our sons to love and respect people and to look for a wife who fears the Lord.

Oh, but you say, *I fall so short.* Yes, so do we all. This is cause for repentance, not resignation. The gospel offers forgiveness for our failures and makes true and lasting change possible. None of us will ever be a perfect example of true beauty to our children, but as we grow in true beauty, we will make a beautiful imprint on our children's lives.

Talk to Our Children about True Beauty

God uses words to tell us about beauty, and we must use words to tell our children about beauty (Deut. 6:6–9; Proverbs 31; Eph. 6:1–4).

First, we need to tell our children of *the beauty of God*. Let's talk to them in simple terms about the beauty of God's character. Even a small child can begin to learn about the beauty of God's sovereignty over the planets and the seasons and the seas, his wisdom in directing our lives, and his goodness in the daily blessings we receive.

Even more important than telling our daughters how beautiful we think *they* are is telling them how beautiful *God* is. Sure, it can be helpful to counteract the degrading messages about women in our culture with biblical teaching about the dignity and beauty of every human being as made in the image of God, but most of all, we want to direct our daughter's attention outward toward God's beauty.

In fact, an overemphasis on our daughters' outward appearance—no matter how affirming—can reinforce their sinful tendencies to vanity and self-focus. More than confidence or security in their own beauty, we want our daughters to be enthralled with God's beauty. When our daughters are captivated by the gospel, they will find freedom and confidence that will rise above all insecurities.

Second, we should talk to our children about the true beauty that is pleasing to God—*the hidden beauty of the heart* (1 Pet. 3:3–6). Let's tell them about the importance of trusting God and doing good works. And point out examples of true beauty. Go on true beauty hunts! Teach them to be keen spotters of true beauty in Scripture, in literature, and in the godly women they know. As we talk often of true beauty, we will be shaping our daughters' aspirations and our sons' opinions of beauty.

We can catechize our children in the beauty of God and the beauty he delights in. For example:

Q. What is true beauty?
A. To behold and reflect the beauty of God.

Q. How does Scripture tell women to reflect the beauty of God?
A. To have a gentle and quiet spirit. (1 Pet. 3:3–6)

Q. What does it mean to have a gentle and quiet spirit?
A. To trust God when life is hard. (1 Pet. 3:3–6)

Q. How else can we become beautiful?
A. By doing good works for God's glory. (1 Tim. 2:9–10)

Q. Who are the women we should want to be like?
A. The holy women of the past who put their hope in God. (1 Pet. 3:3–6)

Q. Who is the kind of woman a man should want to marry?
A. A woman who fears the Lord. (Prov. 31:30)

Third, let's teach our children to recognize *beauty's counter- feit*: charm and outward beauty that are fleeting and deceitful (Prov. 31:30). Our children are desperately in need of discernment. We must train them to identify the false beauty messages of the world that assault them on a moment-by-moment basis. This means, in age-appropriate ways, we begin to talk to them about the unattractiveness of immodesty or vanity that they may observe and encounter. Our words should counteract and undercut our culture's deceitful messages about physical beauty.

Finally, there are *words that are better left unsaid*. Drawing our children into negative dialogue about our appearance—"Do you think Mommy looks fat in this dress?" "Mommy wishes she was young and pretty like you"—will only give ungodly shape to their developing beliefs about beauty. Commenting about others to them—"Can you believe what she was wearing?" "That girl really needs to lose some weight"—is not only unkind but teaches our children to judge others based on outward appearance.

Not only do we need to be careful how we speak to our children about beauty, we also must be careful how we speak in front of them, even when we think they aren't paying attention. Little children have big ears. Conversations with our husbands or with a girlfriend, or mutterings to ourselves that communicate an unbiblical message about beauty can all make an outsized impression on our children.

Also, we do not serve our daughters by dropping subtle hints (which are never as subtle as we think) about their appearance. If we observe that a daughter needs to change her eating habits or care for her appearance in a more God-glorifying manner, then we can provide practical diet help or graciously show her how Scripture should influence her beauty pursuit. But nagging and carping will only stoke discouragement or resentment.

By contrast, as our daughters grow older, humble and age-appropriate admission of our own struggles with beauty can go a long way toward helping them make progress in their own pursuit of true beauty. As we help our daughters see how we are seeking to apply God's truth, we can impart to them the discernment and conviction they need.

Guard Our Children for True Beauty

In addition to talking about true beauty, we must protect our children from the influence of our culture's false and destructive messages about beauty.

Guard their heroes. Children collect heroes: people or characters they want to be like. This means that we as parents must watch over and wisely supervise our children's affections. Who are our child's heroes? Who do they admire and try to imitate? Often, children's first heroes are the characters they see on television or the toys they play with. As they grow older, they may look to athletes, actors, or musicians. These personalities can shape the development of their desires and beliefs in profound ways.

As our children identify with these heroes—wanting to dress like them, talk like them, be like them—they imbibe the messages about beauty that these characters display. Consider: what do the TV, music, and toys you allow in your home say about the beauty of God and the true beauty he requires? Do the characters in your children's favorite television shows flaunt their immodesty or vanity? Do the toys they play with promote an ungodly perspective of physical beauty? As parents, let's wisely help our children choose their heroes.

Guard their childhood. Children are beautiful, largely because they don't know it yet. A young girl is fascinated by the world, not trying to fascinate others with how she looks. This lack of self-awareness is a gift from God and meant to be enjoyed. But sometimes, as parents, we prematurely interrupt our daughters' blissful ignorance by paying excessive attention to how they look.

Let's seek to guard our daughters' childhood instead of following the cultural trend to prematurely rush young girls into womanhood. Be discerning about your daughter's unique temptations to vanity and self-focus. Intentionally limit the time, money, and conversation you spend (or allow them to spend) on their appearance. If necessary, consider delaying certain beauty enhancements such as jewelry or cosmetics. Focus their attention on God and others. Start out as you mean for them to go on.

Guard their friendships. True friends teach us to love true beauty. Conversely, vain and self-focused friends may encourage those sinful tendencies already at work in our hearts. A wise mother will carefully watch over her daughter's friendships. Consider: what do your daughter and her friends talk about most when they are together? What are their favorite hobbies and activities? Does time with friends make her more consumed with herself, with the latest styles, with being physically beautiful? Let's help our daughters choose friends wisely and become the kind of friend who influences others to serve and to obey God. This may mean limiting the time two girls spend together, or taking a more proactive role in choosing their activities when they are together.

As moms we should seek to create a culture of friendship between our daughters and their friends that promotes and cultivates true beauty. Friendships that are built around trusting God and doing good works will help our daughters grow up to be truly beautiful.

Conclusion

Raising our daughters to be truly beautiful and teaching our sons to prize true beauty won't be easy. It requires effort to model and talk about true beauty and to guard our children's hearts from worldly messages about beauty. But God has promised to help as we take steps of faith and obedience, seeking to raise children who understand and strive after the beauty that is pleasing to him. May God give us grace to pass on a legacy of true beauty to the next generation.

Study Guide

Chapter 1:
True Beauty and Our Culture

1. How have you observed our culture's obsession with physical beauty? Why do you think our culture is so fixated on how we look?

2. In what ways is the message of God's Word in Proverbs 31:30 different from the message we receive from the world around us about beauty?

3. What is one of your biggest struggles with beauty? Would you describe your struggles with beauty as "low-grade" or "all-consuming"? Why?

4. What is the gospel according to physical beauty? In what ways have you believed that physical beauty would bring you happiness or a better life? Has it delivered as promised?

5. What do you hope you will learn about the Bible and true beauty from this book? What struggle with beauty do you hope this book will address?

Chapter 2:
True Beauty and Our God

1. Describe a quality of God's beauty you recently read about in Scripture or observed in creation.

2. How does God's beauty transform how we see ourselves and others?

3. What is one of your favorite ways to express your taste for beauty? How does making ourselves or our surroundings beautiful reflect the beauty of God?

4. What was the effect of Adam and Eve's sin on humankind's vision of beauty? In what ways do you see this played out in your own life and in the culture around us?

5. How does the gospel lay double claim to our taste for beauty? What implication does this have for your life?

6. Who or what most influences your style? What is one step you can take to limit worldly influence on your taste for beauty?

7. What is one aspect of God's beauty that you would like to more truly reflect and honor in your taste for beauty? How can you do this?

Chapter 3:
True Beauty and Our Hearts

1. Who do you find yourself identifying with more—April or Eva? How so?

2. Why do our struggles with beauty seem to perpetually resurface? Why does the "you are beautiful just the way you are" counsel not go far enough?

3. How is low self-esteem the flip side of vanity? In what ways have you seen this in your own life?

4. If vanity is to take pride in our looks and to try to get attention, approval, or admiration for some aspect of our appearance, how are you tempted to be vain?

5. How are "trying to get attention for how we look" and "moping because we don't get attention" both attempts to rob God of glory?

6. What must we understand in order to begin to break free from our beauty struggles? How is beholding the beauty of God the antidote to self-glory?

Chapter 4:
True Beauty and Our Bodies

1. Describe a handmade item that is special to you. How does it help you appreciate the handiwork of God in creating your body?

2. In what ways are you are tempted to complain about your appearance? How does the truth that you are "fearfully and wonderfully made" by God put your complaints in a different light?

3. How can we accept our bodies with gratefulness to our Creator without becoming self-focused?

4. In what ways can our eating and exercising become a pursuit of self-glory? How have you experienced this in your own life?

5. How does stewarding our bodies for service to Christ transform our perspective on weight and our decisions about how much to eat and exercise? What is one way you can apply this truth?

6. Which consideration—your heart, safety, others—do you want to apply to your beauty-enhancing choices? How can you do this?

Chapter 5:
True Beauty and Our Clothes

1. Why are we often unclear, indifferent, or legalistic in our approach to clothing? Why must we not ignore this topic?

2. How does the biblical definition of modesty settle "The Line Question"?

3. What role does the culture play in influencing our understanding of modesty?

4. How do we know if we are guilty of being excessive or seductive in our dress? What is one way you are tempted to spend inordinate time, money, or effort on your appearance?

5. What is "respectable apparel" and what is it not?

6. How can we imitate the loveliness of Christ without seeking to draw attention to ourselves with our clothes?

Chapter 6:
True Beauty and Our Trust

1. How does the biblical definition of a gentle and quiet spirit differ from the stereotype? How is the gentle woman a strong woman?

2. In what ways can the justice and kindness of God help us respond with a gentle and quiet spirit when we experience mistreatment from others for how we look?

3. What are ways that we as women are tempted to compare ourselves? How does trusting God help us to resist comparison and sinful envy?

4. What difference will it make in our marriages if trust in God, and not our beauty, is the foundation of our hope?

5. How does the truth that God—not man or our physical beauty—determines our future help us to have a gentle and quiet spirit in the midst of extended singleness?

6. In what ways is God's perspective of aging contrary to our culture's view? How does God's Word transform our attitude toward growing old?

7. What is one way you want to apply God's true beauty regimen this week by trusting him for a specific beauty-related trial or temptation?

Chapter 7:
True Beauty and Our Works

1. How do good works make us beautiful "reflectors of Christ"?

2. Describe a woman you know who has a reputation for good works. How do her good works make her beautiful?

3. If we are all to strive for a reputation of good works in order to reflect the beauty of the Savior's good work, what is one good work from the list in chapter 7 that you would like to put into practice?

4. Who is the most truly beautiful woman you know? Why?

5. How does the anticipation of seeing Christ in his beauty transform our pursuit of beauty today?

6. What is one way that you want to grow in true beauty—*to behold and reflect the beauty of God*?

Notes

Chapter 1: True Beauty and Our Culture

1. *Girltalk* can be found at www.girltalkhome.com.

2. "Madonna's Exercise Regime: How Much Is Too Much?," *MSN UK*, August 19, 2009, http://style.uk.msn.com/health/articles.aspx?cp-documentid=149248773.

3. Jonathon Morgan, "Jennifer Aniston Spends $20,000 a Month on Her Beauty Routine," *Stylelist*, July 17, 2008, http://main.stylelist.com/2008/07/17/jennifer-aniston-spends-20-000-a-month-on-her-beauty-routine/.

4. Susan Stamberg, "Beauty Series, Part 2: Pitching Beauty to Teens," *NPR* online, June 22, 2004, http://www.npr.org/templates/story/story.php?storyId=1968820.

5. Molly Faulkner-Bond, "Why Vanity Keeps Women Poor," *BlogHer* (blog), accessed June 9, 2013, http://www.blogher.com/why-vanity-keeps-us-poor.

6. Nancy Etcoff, *Survival of the Prettiest: The Science of Beauty* (New York: Anchor Books, 2000), 6.

7. Kate Randall, "That's a LOT of Slap! Women Spend a Year and Three Months of Their Lives Applying Make-up," *Mail Online*, February 20, 2013, http://www.dailymail.co.uk/femail/article-2281621/Thats-LOT-mirror-time-Women-spend-year-lives-applying-make-up.html.

8. Ellie Krupnick, "Average Time Spent Shaving Legs in a Lifetime? 72 Days, New Survey Says," *Huffington Post*, April 11, 2013, http://www.huffingtonpost.com/2013/04/11/average-time-spent-shaving-legs_n_3063127.html.

9. "100 Million Dieters, $20 Billion: The Weight-Loss Industry by the Numbers," *ABC News* online, May 8, 2012, http://abcnews.go.com/Health/100-million-dieters-20-billion-weight-loss-industry/story?id=16297197.

10. "Get the Facts on Eating Disorders," NEDA, accessed June 9, 2013, http://www.nationaleatingdisorders.org/get-facts-eating-disorders.

11. "65% of Women in U.S. Have Eating Disorders," *NewsMedical*, April 22, 2008, http://www.news-medical.net/news/2008/04/22/37616.aspx.

12. "Quick Facts: Highlights of the ASAPS 2012 Statistics on Cosmetic Surgery," The American Society for Aesthetic Plastic Surgery, accessed April 23, 2013, http://www.surgery.org/sites/default/files/2012-quickfacts.pdf.

13. Quoted in Albert Mohler, "A Christian Vision of Beauty, Part Three," *AlbertMohler.com*, November 18, 2005, http://www.albertmohler.com/2005/11/18/a-christian-vision-of-beauty-part-three/.

14. Albert Mohler, "A Christian Vision of Beauty, Part Three."

15. Stephen M. Silverman, "Halle Berry: Beauty Can't Stop Heartache," *People.com*, August 3, 2004, http://www.people.com/people/article/0,,675350,00.html.

16. Bruce K. Waltke, *The Book of Proverbs, Chapters 15–31,* New International Commentary on the New Testament (Grand Rapids, MI: Eerdmans, 2005), 535.

17. Charles Bridges, *An Exposition of the Book of Proverbs* (New York: R. Carter, 1847), 532.

18. Waltke, *The Book of Proverbs, Chapters 15–31*, 535.

19. David Powlison, "Your Looks: What the Voices Say and the Images Portray," *The Journal of Biblical Counseling* 15, no. 2 (1997): 41.

20. Bridges, *An Exposition of the Book of Proverbs*, 532.

Chapter 2: True Beauty and Our God

1. Emma Gray, "The 'Perfect Woman' In 1912, Elsie Scheel, Was 171 Pounds And Loved Beefsteaks," *Huffington Post*, December 26, 2012, http://www.huffingtonpost.com/2012/12/26/perfect-woman-1912_n_2365529.html.

2. Tamara Abraham, "'Add 5lb of Solid Flesh in a Week!' The Vintage Ads Promoting Weight GAIN," *Mail Online*, November 30, 2011, http://www.dailymail.co.uk/femail/article-2067821/Add-5lb-solid-flesh-week-The-vintage-ads-promoting-weight-GAIN.html.

3. Monica Hesse and Dan Zak, "The List: 2012," *The Washington Post* online, December 28, 2012, http://www.washingtonpost.com/wp-srv/artsandliving/features/2011/year-in-review/the-list.html.

4. Jonathan Edwards, *Sermons and Discourses, 1720–1723,* ed. Wilson H. Kimnach, The Works of Jonathan Edwards 10 (New Haven, CT: Yale University Press, 1992), 15.

5. Wayne Grudem, *Systematic Theology: An Introduction to Biblical Doctrine* (Grand Rapids, MI: Zondervan, 1994), 1236.

6. C. S. Lewis, *Till We Have Faces: A Myth Retold* (Orlando, FL: Harcourt, 1980), 75.

7. Sam Storms, "The Ultimate Aim of Theology," *Enjoying God* (blog), February 21, 2006, http://www.samstorms.com/all-articles/post/the-ultimate-aim-of-theology.

8. Steve DeWitt, *Eyes Wide Open: Enjoying God in Everything* (Grand Rapids, MI: Credo House, 2012), 60.

9. Grudem, *Systematic Theology*, 442.

10. Albert Mohler, "The Snare of Beauty—Flashpoints of Our Obsession with Attractiveness," *AlbertMohler.com*, July 22, 2010, http://www.albertmohler.com/2010/07/22/the-snare-of-beauty-flashpoints-of-our-obsession-with-attractiveness/.

11. Leland Ryken, James C. Wilhoit, and Tremper Longman III, eds., *Dictionary of Biblical Imagery* (Downers Grove, IL: InterVarsity Press, 1998), 85.

12. Ibid., 82.

13. John Angell James, *Female Piety* (New York: Robert Carter & Brothers, 1854), 305–6.

14. Tim Keller, "Encountering Jesus: A look at his Claims and Character," *Redeemer.com*, http://discover.redeemer.com/Jesus/63/read.

15. Timothy Keller, *The Grieving Sisters* (New York: Dutton, 2013), loc. 170.

16. Matthew Bridges, "Crown Him with Many Crowns," 1851, *Hymnsite.com*, http://www.hymnsite.com/lyrics/umh327.sht.

17. Grudem, *Systematic Theology*, 222.

Chapter 3: True Beauty and Our Hearts

1. Edward T. Welch, *When People Are Big and God Is Small: Overcoming Peer Pressure, Codependency, and the Fear of Man* (Phillipsburg, NJ: P&R, 1997), 32.

2. Jonathan Edwards, *Sermons and Discourses, 1720–1723,* ed. Wilson H. Kimnach, The Works of Jonathan Edwards 10 (New Haven, CT: Yale University Press, 1992), 417.

3. Caroline Weerstra, *Westminster Shorter Catechism for Kids: Workbook One (Questions 1–10): Who Is God?* (Schenectady, NY: Common Life Press, 2011), 10. Emphasis added.

4. Paul David Tripp, *Instruments in the Redeemer's Hands: People in Need of Change Helping People in Need of Change* (Phillipsburg, NJ: P&R, 2002), 34–35.

5. J. I. Packer, *Praying the Lord's Prayer* (Wheaton, IL: Crossway, 2007), 114.

6. C. S. Lewis, *The Collected Letters of C. S. Lewis*, vol. 3: *Narnia, Cambridge, and Joy, 1950–1963* (New York: HarperOne, 2007), 429.

7. G. K. Chesterton, *Orthodoxy* (Hollywood, CA: Simon & Brown, 2013), 17.

8. Ed Welch, *Does Thin Equal Beautiful? A Biblical Vision of Beauty* (sermon, Capitol Hill Baptist Church, Washington, DC, Feb. 3, 2006), http://www.capitolhillbaptist .org/audio/2006/02/does-thin-equal-beautiful/.

9. John Piper, "Her Body, Her Self, and Her God," *Desiring God*, October 28, 1997, http://www.desiringgod.org/resource-library/taste-see-articles/her-body-her-self -and-her-god?lang=en.

Chapter 4: True Beauty and Our Bodies

1. Story adapted from Carolyn Mahaney, "True Beauty," in *Biblical Womanhood in the Home*, ed. Nancy Leigh DeMoss (Wheaton, IL: Crossway, 2002), 41–42.

2. Jerry Bridges, *Trusting God: Even When Life Hurts*, 2nd ed. (Colorado Springs, CO: NavPress, 2008), 154.

3. Ibid., 156.

4. George MacDonald, quoted in ibid., 157.

5. Elisabeth Elliot, *Discipline: The Glad Surrender* (Grand Rapids, MI: Revell, 2006), 44.

6. Debra Evans, *Beauty and the Best* (Colorado Springs, CO: Focus on the Family; distr. by Word Books, 1993), 182–83.

7. "65% of Women in U.S. Have Eating Disorders," *NewsMedical*, April 22, 2008, http://www.news-medical.net/news/2008/04/22/37616.aspx.

8. For further reading, see Edward Welch, *Eating Disorders* (Greensboro, NC: New Growth Press, 2008).

9. "O for a Thousand Tongues to Sing," Charles Wesley, 1739.

10. Clifford Bassett, "Killer Eyelashes? Latest Beauty Craze Linked to Severe Allergies, Infections," *FoxNews.com*, May 9, 2013, http://www.foxnews.com/health/2013/05 /09/killer-eyelashes-latest-beauty-craze-could-cause-severe-allergies/.

Chapter 5: True Beauty and Our Clothes

1. Robert G. Spinney, *Dressed to Kill: Thinking Biblically about Modest & Immodest Clothing* (Hartsville, TN: Tulip Books, 2007), 7.

2. Thomas R. Schreiner, *The New American Commentary*, vol. 37, *1, 2 Peter, Jude* (Nashville, TN: Holman Reference, 2003), 153–54.

3. George W. Knight III, *The Pastoral Epistles*, New International Greek Testament Commentary, eds. I. Howard Marshall and W. Ward Gasque (Grand Rapids, MI: Eerdmans,1999), 136. Emphasis added.

4. James B. Hurley, quoted in John R. W. Stott, *Guard the Truth: The Message of 1 Timothy & Titus* (Downers Grove, IL: InterVarsity Press, 1996), 136.

5. Knight, *Pastoral Epistles*, 136. Emphasis added.

6. "Ten Years In," *This American Life*, September 9, 2011, http://www.thisamericanlife.org/radio-archives/episode/445/ten-years-in.

7. Knight, *Pastoral Epistles*, 134; John F. MacArthur, *First Timothy,* MacArthur New Testament Commentary (Chicago: Moody, 1995), 81.

8. Knight, *Pastoral Epistles*, 134.

9. Spinney, *Dressed to Kill*, 81.

10. C. J. Mahaney, ed., *Worldliness: Resisting the Seduction of a Fallen World* (Wheaton, IL: Crossway, 2008), 119.

11. Ibid., 121.

12. Spinney, *Dressed to Kill*, 6.

13. Ibid., 16.

14. MacArthur, *First Timothy*, 81.

15. Rachel Lee Carter, *Fashioned by Faith* (Nashville, TN: Thomas Nelson, 2011), 1–2.

16. Nancy Leigh DeMoss, *The Look: Does God Really Care What I Wear?* (Buchanan, MI: Revive Our Hearts, 2003), 26.

17. Stott, *Guard the Truth*, 83.

Chapter 6: True Beauty and Our Trust

1. Peter H. Davids, *The First Epistle of Peter*, 2nd ed. (Grand Rapids, MI: Eerdmans, 1990), 118.

2. Ibid., 119.

3. Ibid.

4. *ESV Study Bible*, "Introduction to the First Epistle of Peter" (Wheaton, IL: Crossway, 2008), 2403.

5. John Piper, "He Trusted to Him Who Judges Justly," *Desiring God*, August 25, 1991, http://www.desiringgod.org/resource-library/sermons/he-trusted-to-him-who-judges-justly?lang=en.

6. Ibid.

7. Iain H. Murray, *Jonathan Edwards: A New Biography* (Carlisle, PA: Banner of Truth, 1987), 327.

8. Jonathan Edwards, *Charity and Its Fruits: Christian Love as Manifested in the Heart and Life*, ed. Tryon Edwards, repr. ed. (Carlisle, PA: Banner of Truth, 1969), 79–80.

9. Elisabeth Elliot, *The Path of Loneliness: Finding Your Way through the Wilderness to God* (Ada, MI: Revell, 2007), 32.

10. Thomas R. Schreiner, *The New American Commentary,* vol. 37, *1, 2 Peter, Jude* (Nashville, TN: Holman Reference, 2003), 155.

Chapter 7: True Beauty and Our Works

1. LaNae Valentine, "Beauty Extremes," Recapturing Beauty, accessed June 9, 2013, https://recapturingbeauty.byu.edu/topics/timeline.php.

2. Ibid.

3. "Mascara," *Wikipedia, the Free Encyclopedia*, June 3, 2013, http://en.wikipedia.org/w/index.php?title=Mascara&oldid=558054376.

4. Robin Marantz Henig, "The Price of Perfection," *The Journal of Biblical Counseling* 15, no. 2 (Winter 1997).

5. Jerry Bridges, *The Practice of Godliness: Godliness Has Value for All Things*, rev. ed. (Colorado Springs, CO: NavPress, 1996), 190.

6. Martyn Lloyd-Jones, *Studies in the Sermon on the Mount* (Grand Rapids, MI: Eerdmans, 1984), 179.

7. Robert G. Spinney, *Dressed to Kill: Thinking Biblically about Modest & Immodest Clothing* (Hartsville, TN: Tulip Books, 2007), 8.

8. Spinney, *Dressed to Kill*, 8.

9. Amy Raper, quoted in Pat Ennis and Lisa Tatlock, *Practicing Hospitality: The Joy of Serving Others* (Wheaton, IL: Crossway, 2008), 53.

10. John Piper, "Strategic Hospitality," *Desiring God*, August 25, 1985, http://www .desiringgod.org/resource-library/sermons/strategic-hospitality?lang=en.

11. Walter Lock, *A Critical and Exegetical Commentary on the Pastoral Epistles: I & II Timothy and Titus* (New York: Continuum International, 1924), 57.

12. Charles H. Spurgeon, *Beside Still Waters: Words of Comfort for the Soul*, ed. Roy H. Clarke (Nashville, TN: Thomas Nelson, 1999), 9.

13. Charles H. Spurgeon, "Abraham's Double Blessing" (sermon, Metropolitan Tabernacle Pulpit, November 8, 1885), http://www.spurgeongems.org/vols43-45 /chs2523.pdf.

14. Albert Mohler, "A Christian Vision of Beauty, Part Three," *AlbertMohler.com*, November 18, 2005, http://www.albertmohler.com/2005/11/18/a-christian-vision -of-beauty-part-three/.

15. Ibid.

Scripture Index

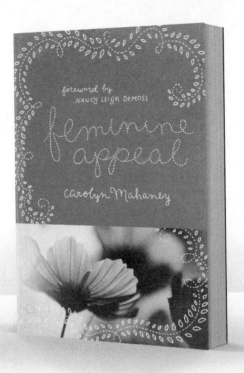

Learn to live with true
feminine appeal
... and become a woman who lives for God.

"Offers the mature mentoring that women of every age yearn for. This may be an excellent stand-in for the mentor you lack, or it will wonderfully complement the relationship you already have."

John and Noël Piper, desiringGod.org

"We'll give this book our ultimate endorsement—we have given it to all our married daughters!"

Dennis and Barbara Rainey, founders of *Family Life Today*

"Helps women recover the nearly lost treasure of God's way of thinking and living."

Nancy Leigh DeMoss, host of *Revive Our Hearts* radio program

Struggling to do it all without feeling overwhelmed?

"Like most women today, I struggle with feelings of 'too much to do and too little time to do it'! My friend Carolyn Mahaney, along with her daughters, offers practical, biblical advice to help us plan, evaluate, strategize, and make wise choices concerning our time and priorities."

Nancy Leigh DeMoss, host of *Revive Our Hearts* radio program

"This book offers no simplistic solutions to the perils of superwoman syndrome. Instead, it deliberately leads women to the bedrock of biblical priorities and then suggests real-life methods by which to apply them."

Mary K. Mohler, wife of R. Albert Mohler Jr., president of The Southern Baptist Theological Seminary

How to Become a Godly Woman
A Conversation for Mothers and Daughters

Mothers and daughters have a lot to talk about. That's how God designed it. A mother is her daughter's first role model, teacher, and friend, and she carries the responsibility of passing on to her daughter a legacy of biblical womanhood.

Join mother-daughter team Carolyn Mahaney and Nicole Whitacre as they give you insights and suggestions on how to talk—really *talk*—to each other about what it means to become a godly woman.

For more information, visit crossway.org.